To dear W████

May your inner weather
of spirit continue to
blossom in love and
prosperity !

With richest blessings,

Ernest Ch█

4/01/09

Wendy

PRAISE FOR *SOUL CURRENCY*

"There are prosperity teachers who talk abundance and millionaires who walk abundance. Ernest Chu is a millionaire prosperity teacher who walks his talk. In *Soul Currency*, he'll show you how you can do that, too."

— Cary Bayer, author of *The Prosperity Aerobics*

"*Soul Currency* is a delightful and important book for anyone who wants to create both inner and outer prosperity. Ernest Chu shares from the heart and uplifts the reader with his guidance and wisdom."

— Barbara De Angelis, PhD,
author of the #1 *New York Times* bestseller *How Did I Get Here?*

"Absolutely soul savvy! A practical, thought-provoking, and certainly inspirational book that will infuse your spiritual essence into your material existence. Finally, true abundance can be yours."

— Dr. John F. Demartini, author of *How to Make One Hell of a Profit
and Still Get to Heaven*, featured in the movie *The Secret*

"Ernest Chu is the perfect person to write a book about spiritual wealth and financial health. Descended from a legendary Confucian grand master, he has years of experience and the modern-world skills of a billion-dollar investment banker. Ernie has written an exceptional book that shows you how to invest your inner wealth to create purpose and prosperity in your life. His healthy prescription for a fulfilling and abundant life will truly change your life."

— Terry Shintani, MD, bestselling author of *The Hawaii Diet*
and *The Good Carbohydrate Revolution*

"Ernest Chu's easy-to-learn concepts will teach you to powerfully unleash your inner capital, keep your spiritual and material bank accounts filled to the brim, and let your soul prosper."

— Jason Oman, coauthor of *Conversations with Millionaires*

"Grounded in ancient spiritual principles, Ernest Chu's *Soul Currency* is the perfect modern and practical guide to living a prosperous life."

— Chris Michaels, founder of the Center for Spiritual Living in Kansas City,
Missouri, and author of *Your Soul's Assignment*

"As an investment banker, Ernest Chu is brilliant. As a teacher of ancient wisdom and universal principles, he is a master. When you blend these together and put them in a book, you have *Soul Currency*. Ernie is a guide we can trust because he has already been where he wants to lead us. . . . He has scouted the terrain and makes the journey to a life truly worth living not only enjoyable but obtainable. That's my kind of teacher."

— Dennis Merritt Jones, DD, author of
The Art of Being — 101 Ways to Practice Purpose in Your Life

"In *Soul Currency*, Ernie Chu explains the connection between your soul currency and creating prosperity. I highly recommend this dynamic book."

— Hale Dwoskin, author of the *New York Times* bestseller *The Sedona Method*

"Real money is an illusion; soul currency is real! Everyone on the planet needs to read this book and embrace the principles it contains. . . . By doing so we would all be able to open our hearts so that we could see the many gifts and strengths we have in our 'spiritual pocketbooks.' We would realize our true worth and transform it into cash in hand. An absolutely spectacular read — again and again!"

— Karen Simmons, founder and CEO of Autism Today and coauthor of *Chicken Soup for the Soul: Children with Special Needs*

"Having been the CFO of publicly held companies, Reverend Ernest Chu has the perfect background to blend the spiritual principles of prosperity with the wisdom of sound financial practices. *Soul Currency* will help you discover what turns you on, and then help you to turn it on. It will assist you in living a fulfilling life while being in the affluent flow of Spirit."

— Dr. Christian Sorensen, author of *Catch the Spirit* and founding community leader of the United Church of Religious Science

"I love *Soul Currency*. Ernest Chu offers practical and easy steps to manifest your dreams and create inner and outer wealth. Savor the advice and insights; add flow and the richness of purpose to your life."

— Sandy Grason, international speaker and author of *Journalution: Journaling to Awaken Your Inner Voice, Heal Your Life, and Manifest Your Dreams*

"This beautiful, heartfelt, easy-to-read book offers a refreshingly insightful path to abundance and fulfillment. You will discover a path to prosperity rooted in love and creativity rather than desire and greed. You will learn that the magnificent abundance you seek is already within you. I highly recommend Ernest Chu, and I highly recommend this wonderful book!"

— John E. Welshons, author of *Awakening from Grief* and *When Prayers Aren't Answered*

"*Soul Currency* is a powerful message of hope. Developing one's spiritual attributes to the fullest assures a rich, rewarding life, filled with joy, happiness, and economic independence. Ernest Chu's crystal-clear message in *Soul Currency* will help a wide range of people find relevance and meaning in their lives. It's a great message and should be told."

— Michael A. Stephen, retired chairman of Aetna Insurance and author of *Spirituality in Business*

SOUL CURRENCY

SOUL CURRENCY

Investing Your Inner Wealth
for Fulfillment & Abundance

ERNEST D. CHU

NEW WORLD LIBRARY
NOVATO, CALIFORNIA

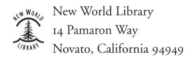 New World Library
14 Pamaron Way
Novato, California 94949

Text design by Tona Pearce Myers

Library of Congress Cataloging-in-Publication Data
Chu, Ernest D.
Soul currency : investing your inner wealth for fulfillment and abundance / Ernest D. Chu.
  p.   cm.
Includes bibliographical references and index.
ISBN 978-1-57731-624-4 (hbk. : alk. paper)
 1. Job satisfaction—Social aspects. 2. Entrepreneurship—Social aspects.
3. Success in business—Social aspects. 4. Success. 5. Self-realization. I. Title.
HF5549.5.J63C477 2008
650.1—dc22   2008026544

First printing, October 2008
North American edition ISBN 978-1-57731-624-4
International paperback edition ISBN 978-1-57731-652-7

Printed in the United States on 50% postconsumer-waste recycled paper

g New World Library is a proud member of the Green Press Initiative.

10 9 8 7 6 5 4 3 2 1

To the memory of my grandfather, T. C. Chu,
who always insisted that I would be a writer,
even before I turned six years old,
and who insisted I read Plutarch's Lives *when I was twelve*

To the special memory of my late father, Philip,
and mother, Esther,
who always saw that writing was a passion for me

To my brother, Jim,
who has helped me more
than he could ever know

To my sons, Christopher and Jonathan,
who are my teachers

CONTENTS

7. SOUL CURRENCY "MAGIC"

Living in the Flow   193

INTRODUCTION

What Is Soul Currency?

Your work is to discover your work and then with all your heart
give yourself to it.

— BUDDHA

Seated at a table in a restaurant, we looked into each other's
eyes. I listened with empathy as my friend spoke to me about
the financial hardships he faced and how he just wasn't happy.
Frustrated and angry, he was tired of making an effort to change
his lot in life. Although he felt he had something more to offer
the world, something truly valuable deep inside him, he wasn't
sure how to reach or express this greatness — and he didn't believe anyone especially cared or wanted him to try. He had come
to me for my counsel.

In recent years, I have sat at many tables and heard many
comparable tales about bankruptcies, dead-end jobs, heartache,
unrealized dreams, and treadmills of debt. Even people I've spoken with who are getting by financially have often told me they
feel as if the challenge of making ends meet is an obstacle to
greater wealth, joy, and fulfillment. My practical advice to my

friend in the restaurant, and to the others, was the same: "Open to receive."

In my experience, what holds people back from extraordinary success and happiness, what prevents them from creating abundant wealth for themselves and their families, is their underlying sense that they don't deserve more than they have. Being able to receive is directly connected to our self-esteem. It's not that most people think they are worthless, but that they believe they merit, or have the capability of achieving, only a certain level of prosperity. This stymies their efforts. Their uncertainty arises in the process of discovering how to do something they truly love in a smart enough way to bring in a considerable amount of money. So they don't risk it. They do the best they can and reserve doing what they love for the weekends. Or they funnel most of their creative energy into giving to others, making charitable efforts and loving gestures that bring them a sense of greater well-being yet leave them feeling drained of energy. They settle for the discomfort of limitations and a degree of deprivation.

You and I do not know each other, and yet I believe you are a good, hardworking person. I'd like to think that if we met we would be friends. I cannot presume to know or understand the past or current circumstances of your life. You may be old or young, male or female, rich or poor, married or single, happy or sad. Nor do I know the nature of your sweetest dreams and grandest ambitions. You may be an inventor, a real estate agent, an actor, or a lawyer. However, I invite you to sit with me as you read this book, and open your mind to receive ideas, cultivate your passion, and expand the richness and vibrancy of your life.

If you were here beside me now, I would look you in the eyes, perhaps take your hands in mine, and we'd discuss the wondrous, creative callings of our hearts and the true nature of fulfillment and enlightened wealth. I would assure you, as I did my friend some years ago, that the world most definitely needs your greatness, even hungers for it. That's why those who learn to receive love, and then allow it to flow through them from an inner sense of sufficiency, tend to be handsomely rewarded.

SOUL CURRENCY MEETS WALL STREET

Soul Currency is more than just another prosperity or fulfillment book. It is grounded by the more than thirty-five years of experience I've had as a Wall Street investment banker, a member of the New York Stock Exchange, a venture capitalist, and a financial executive in a public company. But it is also rooted in my transformative spiritual journey and my years as a spiritual teacher and minister. This journey led me to become aware of the soul currency that exists within us, and of how to explain, develop, and use it.

The term *soul currency* has two meanings. First, it's a medium for exchanging value. Like money, soul currency can be shared, traded, donated, and invested. But unlike money, it is not a symbolic object. It is spiritual energy that resides in everyone. Each of us embodies this energy in our own unique form. Second, just as the word *current* refers to streaming movements of air, water, or electricity, *soul currency* describes the circulation of the God force through our lives. Is your divine flow a trickle or a gushing fountain?

In this transformative book, I share important techniques and perspectives developed to bridge the material world of finance with the invisible world of Spirit. I'll explain how to tap into the unlimited energy of your soul and boost its circulation. By taking the steps outlined here, you can immediately and consciously begin to draw upon the immense creative power and value of your innermost spiritual resources.

At twenty-five, I became a member of the New York Stock Exchange, one of the oldest and most prestigious institutions in the world. I held the title of senior vice president of a vibrant Wall Street investment bank. Every day a large part of the world's money swirled around me, and I was absorbed in the activity of investing millions of dollars with just a phone call or the click of a mouse.

I am the child of immigrant Chinese parents who came to America to go to college. After World War II broke out and they couldn't return to China, they married. My father took a job in Canada, so my parents relocated for several years, and then managed to come back to America after the war to finish school. Faced with the prospect of going home and having to live in uncertainty under the new communist regime in China, they chose to build their future here.

My parents had brought with them the values they learned while growing up in Shanghai. They both embodied a very strong work ethic and a belief that a good education was important in getting ahead. But in addition to their belief in money, hard work, and struggle, they also believed you couldn't trust the world, that you always had to be careful, and that you had to be lucky to get ahead. Reflecting their principles, I worked my way through college, became well educated, and grew to love the American dream of fulfillment through things, accomplishments, and expensive vacations.

During my career, I have been a founding member of at least nine companies, five of which are publicly traded. In all, I have been directly or indirectly responsible for raising more than $150 million in financing and creating nearly $1 billion in aggregate market value. But despite my success, my greatest apparent failure is what ultimately helped me discover the power of soul currency. On one fateful Monday, my beliefs about the world all changed.

DARK NIGHT OF THE SOUL

"We're out of money," my business partner said, as if she expected me to write a check and solve the problem. There was silence as I took a deep breath, still in shock that our major financing had crumbled because of some undisclosed negative information about my partner's background. The company, which had only recently been launched in the anticipation of acquiring some type of financial backing, now had endless obligations, many of which I had personally guaranteed. It was as if someone had pulled the rug out from under the operation.

My erstwhile partner sought refuge with her family in another state and shortly afterward filed for personal bankruptcy. But I resisted bankruptcy because it would be a huge black mark against me if in the future I ever wanted to advise companies or seek investors. As a result, I became the target of anyone who had a claim against the company. I found myself responsible for nearly $1 million in personal credit card debt, which I had expected the company to reimburse, in addition to vendor obligations, and notes and leases that had been personally guaranteed.

The experience, which occurred more than fifteen years ago, felt like one of the darkest and most shameful of my life. I had to move out of the beautiful home I was so proud to own, and was consigned to living week to week in one small room in the home of a compassionate stranger. Endless days dragged into exhausting weeks. I found it difficult to maintain even a flickering spark of optimism that somehow I would find a way out of this situation.

One day, in the depths of my despair, I looked down on my bedroom floor and saw a prayer that must have fallen out of one of the books on the shelf. As I knelt down and read the prayer, I felt tears welling up in me, and sobs came in great waves, expressing feelings I had never known were in me. The simple message of the prayer was that I was loved.

The next day, my previous sadness and shame had disappeared, and in their place I felt lightness and clarity. Without my even knowing it, my subsequent prayers for guidance and assistance began to be answered in the exact moment I thought of them.

When I had the thought, "Where have I worked that I had the most fun, made the most money, and felt most highly appreciated?" instantly I visualized the small investment bank where I had become a junior partner. An atmosphere of fun and creativity had pervaded the bank, symbolized by an electronic pinball machine in the waiting room. The firm had grown even larger in the period since my departure. It had been nearly twenty years since I'd worked there. If I contacted them, would they even remember me? I decided to reach out.

ANSWERED PRAYERS

"I was about to send this one back," my former mentor from the investment bank said during my first meeting with him as a newly hired consultant. "My intuition tells me this is going to be a good project, but I can't finance anything I don't understand."

This man, the head of the firm, remembered me with lingering affection, even though we hadn't spoken in more than two decades. His gray hair made him look more distinguished now, and he also looked tired, yet it was as if time had stopped and we had forgotten that he had refused to speak to me for many years after I left the firm for a better opportunity. Now he handed me a large package stuffed with papers that he snatched from his outbox just before the mail was cleared for the day.

And so a company with a radical new design for semiconductor packages was the turning point of both my financial recovery and my spiritual journey. I went to visit the semiconductor-packaging company in Florida. Afterward, based upon my recommendation, my investment-banking mentor decided to take the company public. As part of the deal, the company arranged for me to get some stock options.

The night before the company went public, my mentor called me into the office and told me, "Congratulations — in a year or two when you can sell the stock, you'll be a millionaire."

For most people it would have taken a lifetime to recover from the financial catastrophe I'd endured. Even paying down my debt at the rate of ten thousand dollars a year with interest would have required more than two hundred years to make a dent in the million-dollar principal. Yet I was able to construct the foundation of my turnaround in less than eighteen months, although I did have to wait two years to sell my stock to pay down or settle all my debt obligations. It was clearly the work of Spirit.

Working for the bank, I continued to allow Spirit to unfold in me. In the next year, the Florida company's stock continued to rise, partially as a result of my continued enthusiasm for its prospects and how I communicated it. Then I had the opportunity to become a founding executive of another company and do something similar for its operations. And three years later, I had a third success, merging one company into another corporation whose shares were publicly traded. I was now considered a hot commodity in the venture capital world, and my success drew lots of companies and investors. But this time my commitments would be different.

AN OPPORTUNITY TO WAKE UP

The Chinese term for crisis is *wei ji*, a combination of the words for "danger" and "opportunity." Soon after my crisis began, I understood that what had happened to me was not simply a case of financial and corporate mismanagement but a spiritual wake-up call that had been a long time coming. Such spiritual wake-up calls often take the form of a terrible financial crisis, a rancorous divorce, a devastating injury, or a terminal illness. Since I lived in the financial world, what better way for Spirit to get my attention than with a major financial crisis? Danger snapped its fingers in front of me.

Viewing my loss and subsequent success as an opportunity and a divinely guided life-changing event, I started to tell my story in church meetings and workshops that I conducted in spiritual centers over the next decade. I wanted to inspire others who might be going through similar experiences to trust Spirit. Almost every time I gave a workshop, several people would come up and thank me. "I'm going through this now," they would whisper. "Your story gives me hope."

For many years, I told my story as a way to help others see that a lack of prosperity was a liquidity crisis. Liquidity, from a metaphysical standpoint, is about the flow of energy and loving intention rather than about money. Because of my experience, I realized that flow begins on the inside and moves outward, and that no matter what else may seem to produce prosperity, there is only one source: Spirit.

Gradually my approach shifted from telling the story of "what happened" to sharing how I answered the call of Spirit. I began to see the flow of prosperity as an expression of having learned how to give and receive love, and of consciously creating with enjoyment and fun in the oneness of Spirit. My aim in this book is to guide you through a process that enables you to apply the principles of soul currency that I accidentally stumbled upon.

THE EVOLUTION OF SOUL CURRENCY

Several years ago, when I began testing aspects of the program featured in this book, I watched as my students — even those who initially felt nervous or lacked a background of handling wealth — rapidly grasped familiar financial terms such as *currency*, *property*, and *assets* and translated these into their living equivalents, qualities such as imagination, intuition, and insight. They related to the emotional experience that's inherent in the several-step process outlined in *Soul Currency* and built confidence as they went along. Most began to experience tangible shifts in their spirituality and sense of fulfillment, as well as an increase in their income, a process that continues today.

Wall Street–consciousness rarely intersects with the consciousness of spirituality. Yet one often mirrors the other. Most of us are more comfortable with concepts about things we can see and touch. The prosperity model of soul currency will help shift your mind-set from the material symbols of success to your inner resources.

Embracing this new model of prosperity doesn't necessarily mean you'll have instant success. But it does provide a more constructive framework for day-to-day living that can help you bypass many deeply ingrained beliefs that are keeping you stuck and blocking your fulfillment.

Symbols of value expressed in Wall Street language may bring up some emotional obstacles, such as the fear of not being supported, the sense of needing to struggle to create more, or perhaps a belief in lack and limitation as truth, a belief that "there's not enough to go around" or that "nice guys always finish last." But

I can promise you that, when you begin to address these issues in the spiritual terms of soul currency, the immensely creative world within you will come alive, and you will see the flow of love transforming your intentions into a greater vision of life. Your inner life, I assure you, has unlimited possibilities.

Imagine possessing a kind of currency that was easily exchanged for anything you could envision. Imagine that this currency were unlimited, like the power of Aladdin's genie, and that you had an infinite number of wishes. Imagine also that your currency could be exchanged not only for material things, like money and real estate, but also for positive, intangible outcomes to even your most outrageous dreams. What if this currency could fill your life with love, passion, and satisfaction? And what if this currency would rise in value as you became more aware of it? What if this currency were in circulation all around you all the time?

Does this currency — and its circulatory patterns — really exist? Or is it the figment of some overworked Wall Street banker's imagination? And if it does exist, why doesn't everyone know about it and use it all the time?

In this book you'll be introduced to soul currency, a force that is real, not imaginary. It is inexhaustible, immensely alive, and intangibly organic. This extraordinary currency is an integral part of everything we do, become, and experience. When we use it, even unconsciously, we experience a sense of satisfaction and effortless flow in our lives. We achieve our goals using soul currency, often with results that exceed our expectations. Money, love, and support seem to come easily. The right people seem to magically appear in our lives, and we attract opportunity as if a magnet drew it to us.

Since flow and effortless attraction are a rare, albeit welcome, phenomenon for most of us, typically we assume that there are other explanations for these results, such as luck, hard work, and special skills. When this kind of abundance visits, we may wonder how long our good fortune will last, since we believe predominantly that most good things can't last.

But what if they could? What if consciously using this inner power would allow you to create a life of extraordinary fulfillment and dynamic prosperity? What if you could learn to consciously use this extraordinary resource within you? This book will tell you how to harness the power of soul currency so you can live creatively and experience greater satisfaction, love, and prosperity.

THE SOUL CURRENCY METHOD

Soul Currency demonstrates the steps for listening to your soul's passion, for seeking what fulfills you and serves others, for creating a living by becoming alive with what most delights and interests you, and for creating a prosperous flow of loving energy — soul currency.

Chapter 1 is an overview of the soul currency program and what you can expect when you translate the consciousness of Wall Street — of economics — into the spiritual consciousness of empowerment. More important, it explains how to hear and answer the call of your soul.

In chapter 2, I introduce the concept of spiritual assets. I've organized them into four distinct categories, although there is often overlap. I've created a method to help your mind really grasp how valuable they are. I discuss the various calls of the soul and how these may be different for each person. The soul yearns to have these calls answered.

Chapter 3 discusses how you may activate your spiritual assets with the intention to create spiritual capital. You will learn how spiritual capital is multiplied by love. This chapter continues my discussion about finding what fulfills you, and it helps you identify which impulses truly reflect your passion and which impulses arise instead from ego.

What are the impediments to a fulfilling and prosperous life? In chapter 4, I discuss what I call "counterfeit currency," the false beliefs that we know don't work, but which, like a counterfeit hundred-dollar bill, continue to circulate as if they were real. The real value of soul currency becomes evident when you remove your false beliefs from circulation. Finding fulfillment with prosperity is often a process of subtraction rather than addition.

In chapter 5, we look at the power of manifestation through spiritual "adventureprise." Spirit working through you, like an enlightened entrepreneur, can be used to guide you in creating an actual business or a service, either for-profit or nonprofit. Here you'll learn how you can add your own unique value to this enterprise or choose to be fulfilled by playing a supportive role as a member of a team.

Chapter 6 discusses the power of connection and spiritual intelligence and introduces the concepts of stakeholders and self-organizing and self-connecting principles of quantum physics. The power of spiritual capital formation (and indeed even classic capital formation, which I explain in layperson's terms) comes through a multiplicity of invisible channels. Spiritual capital is created as the flow of the universe moves through you.

Finally, in chapter 7, I explore infinite possibility and infinite Spirit, which may hold greater possibilities for you than you realize. What will life look like when you're fulfilled? I will teach you nine principles for living in the flow of soul currency. Prosperity is the natural result of being in harmony with the Spirit, and you'll see that living with meaning and love are far more important priorities than making money.

A PERFECT BEGINNING

I invite you to trust that *Soul Currency* has come into your hands at the perfect time to bring forth your true magnificence. After you finish reading this book and have completed its exercises and affirmations, you may never look at yourself the same way again. You'll hold yourself in higher esteem and place a higher value on what you bring to life. As a result, you can become fearless when making changes.

That's what happened for the friend I introduced earlier, when he opened himself to receive and transformed his understanding of what he had to offer the world. His relationships improved, his business prospered, and he started enjoying the incredible richness of life. Like him, once you read this book, you will no longer see yourself as an individual standing alone against the world. Instead you'll see yourself as the expression of a great, not-too-silent partner — Spirit — whose flow you'll perceive at every level of your life.

THE FLOW OF SOUL CURRENCY

Experiencing the Infinite Power
of Harmony and Creation

The thought manifests as word. The word manifests as deed. The deed develops into habit. The habit hardens into character. So watch the thought and its ways with care. And let it spring from love, born out of concern for all beings.

— BUDDHA, *Dhammapada*

An old Taoist riddle asks: What can be created, but is not seen? What can multiply, but is one? What is felt, but cannot be touched? This riddle might be best answered with a single phrase: the soul's currency, love, which by its very essence is pure, creative spiritual intelligence.

To understand soul currency, you may have to redefine your relationship to other people and the world around you. It's common for people to feel separated; after all, as individuals, we are separate. Yet there is a bigger picture, an underlying level of connection that you can train yourself to perceive. In order to open yourself to receive more abundantly than you do now, you may have to cultivate an awareness of how your success, happiness, relationships, financial well-being, and physical health include and involve the rest of us. Your good is ours. When you are nourished, your fulfillment benefits others.

It's erroneous to give to others without giving to yourself as well, just as it's mistaken to believe that giving to yourself, that taking care of your own needs and interests, is selfish. When you realize your connection to the world, you strengthen and support yourself in a way that benefits others and strengthens and supports the world. You are the steward of your special qualities and talents. The world would be diminished if it lacked your magnificence.

What does *soul currency* really mean? In everything that exists, there is an intangible spiritual force, an ever-present energy of creation. The term *currency* describes its movement. Like an air current or an electrical current, the divine current is one of the most important patterns in our lives. The more freely divine energy circulates in your life, the happier, more success-filled, more gratifying and rich your life becomes.

At the macro level, your soul's currency is the energy of the universe, which can never be created or destroyed but constantly changes shape, assuming endless combinations of visible and invisible form. Another name for this energy is love, which is the medium, or currency, of your spiritual capital, assets that you can consciously invest in different opportunities by using practical principles of value-added entrepreneurship, which I discuss in this book.

Like money, love can be given and received or it can be withheld. Your effective use of your soul's currency depends on your awareness of its presence and whether you decide to invest it. Love operates according to universal law. Your belief in the immense value of your inner assets will increase as you become more aware of love's real potential and see how it grows when circulated.

There are two meanings of *soul currency* that we need to explore: first, the nature of the energy itself; second, what you can do to encourage it to circulate more effortlessly and abundantly through your enterprises.

LOVE AS THE SOUL'S CREATIVE CURRENCY

Love is the essence of Spirit as it gives of itself. It doesn't actually come from you; rather it moves through you. In the context of soul currency, love should not be confused with an emotion. It is more than the different aspects of well-being and compassion that we feel as it flows through us. Rather it is an unconditional, immensely creative force that connects to all of life. Love is responsive to our thoughts and intentions and is the invisible source of the events, coincidences, and effects in the visible world that we call our life. Your soul is the medium that expresses Spirit. The soul yearns to express itself in meaningful activity.

My longtime friend Richard Shulman, an accomplished jazz and New Age musician from Asheville, North Carolina, expresses love through his unique, flowing musical pieces inspired by his trips to places like Assisi, Italy. His musical soul-portraits of people and animals are Spirit-inspired, and utter bliss and light emanate from him as he performs on two and sometimes even three keyboards.[1]

As defined earlier, love is a form of currency because it can metamorphose into a wealth of possibilities, just as monetary currency flows into, shapes, and flows out from different businesses around the world. But unlike monetary currency, soul currency is alive with intelligence, insight, and the essence of Spirit. Unlike monetary currency, which consists exclusively of one symbol of value being exchanged for another, soul currency is infinite. It can become anything. Soul currency is the common denominator of both the material and the invisible universe. The form it takes is your creation; it depends upon your thoughts and intention.

While we've all heard that money can't buy love, love — soul currency — can help you attract money. My friend and business associate for many years, Peter Yip, founded China.com, China's first major Internet portal. He is now chief executive officer of the CDC Corporation, a publicly-held, thriving, integrated supplier of personnel, customer service, strategic, and other business software that has evolved to become more than just an Internet portal. This skinny, unassuming man might easily be mistaken for a schoolteacher, but colleagues describe him as a "rainmaker," an accolade related to his uncanny ability to walk into a room, meet the six people who can help him most, and know exactly how to work with each of them and how each could work with the others to produce benefits for all. It's a skill and vision that can't be taught but which flows from within.

Peter is a perfect example of how even in the business world, where many people consider cooperation a weakness, it's not what we do that defines us, but what we become. Our soul's currency is visible in each of us when we respond and act authentically.

Faye Harris, a pioneer in recruiting women as agents in the insurance industry, a male-dominated business, remembers one of her most challenging moments and how her love enabled her to resolve the problem she faced. Her agency, one of the fastest growing, with women accounting for nearly 90 percent of the employees, specialized in equipment-leasing insurance and depended heavily on a single well-established insurance company.

It came as a shock to learn that her major insurer had decided to discontinue that special insurance. Immediately she thought, "We'll be out of business." She thought of all the women she had recruited who now were doing as well as or better than some of their male counterparts. She thought of all the sacrifices she had made when she had started the company and all the shared hopes and dreams. Her love for her employees and their families drove her to make phone call after phone call, taking advantage of relationships and calling in favors.

Finally Faye was able to arrange a meeting with the insurer's top-level management people. As she sat at the conference table with them, they asked, "Can you assure us that we won't have losses with your accounts? Can you assure us that there won't be ongoing risks?" These were both questions she had anticipated, and she had decided to answer honestly no matter what the consequences.

"No, I can't guarantee there will be no losses or risks," she said. "The probabilities are low, and we've always had a good history. If you decide to discontinue this insurance line, then you'll put us out of business." She spoke from her heart, knowing that she faced long odds.

When she was finished, the committee thanked her for coming in to make her case. Faye wondered if she had just signed a death warrant for her business and her business family. She felt a sense of sadness, as if it were all over. Perhaps she could have sugarcoated her replies. Would that have changed the outlook? How was she going to tell all the women on her staff who had believed that she would somehow pull this out?

When she got to the parking lot, she saw that one member of the committee had followed her down. Initially she thought she'd forgotten some papers, and then when she saw he wasn't carrying anything, she believed he had come down to console her. This man, head of agency sales, was breathless. "You made your case," he said excitedly. "They're not going to put you out of business. They want more people like you to run their agencies and represent our company."

The insurance agency that Faye Harris founded continues to thrive a decade later, although she sold her interest in it. Women still make up a majority of the agents — nearly 70 percent — a group in which she invested her love.

DRAWING FROM THE SOURCE

Love as a manifesting energy has been described by Sri Chinmoy, a master spiritual teacher, as *savikalpa samadhi*, or the first stage of enlightenment, which is an exalted and glowing state of consciousness that is both deliberate and natural. When we create through the flow of love, we may appear to be creating results as individuals, but we are actually creating from the source of oneness.

Our world appears to be full of duality. There is prosperity, and there is scarcity. The stock market goes up, and then it goes down. There is good, and evil. There is Spirit, and there is the human body. But duality is an illusion.

Quantum physicists have observed the underlying intelligence beneath all creation. Intelligence is embodied by even the smallest subatomic waves or particles, and it imbues them with the ability to reorganize instantaneously, respond to thought, and make a universal connection to other particles no matter what distances are involved.

In *The Science of Mind*, Ernest Holmes writes, "There is a Universal Mind, Spirit and Intelligence that is the origin of everything." He goes on to say that "we are thinking, willing, knowing conscious centers of Life. We are surrounded, immersed in, and there is flowing through us... call it what you will."[2]

In essence, the universe is always answering yes to what we put into it. But we are not simply caught up in the flow of Spirit; we are one with the Spirit flowing through us.

Creative flow is called by many names: inspiration, imagination, and insight, among others. It pours into us in the moments that occur between thoughts and busyness. When author Deepak Chopra spoke at the Broward Center in Fort Lauderdale, Florida in 2006, I heard him say that being in a state of flow is akin to "being in the gap," the timeless space between our thoughts. Soul currency emanates from this space and shows us what to do.

To effectively navigate life in the illusion identified by Hindu sages as the "material world," we must recognize that our creative ability is actually a form of cocreation with the universe that goes beyond anything most of us learned during our upbringing. We live best by following the calls of our souls, because heartfelt intentions activate the flow of creation. This is why the broader meaning of prosperity includes not just financial freedom but also a quality of life that comes from our participation in a supportive and loving world.

Since we are such fundamentally powerful and connected beings, we have a choice to consciously transform our circumstances and prosper. Why not create meaningful work and, with it, enjoy the laughter, the fun, and the ingenuity of Spirit, as well as increased financial rewards? Ernest Holmes says it best: "When we learn to trust the Universe, we shall be happy, prosperous, and well."[3]

THE RESTLESS SPIRIT AT WORK

Our jobs are important to us: they occupy most of our waking hours, and our thoughts about them sometimes even intrude on our sleep. It has been estimated that we work (as opposed to play) at our jobs for nine to ten hours a day, and even more if we take into account the time we spend preparing to go to work, traveling to and from work, and unwinding from work.[4] For the 30–35 million people who are self-employed or who telecommute, there are often periods in which work never ends, even on weekends.[5] We give so much of ourselves to our work, but at the end of life, no one ever says, "I should have spent more time at the office."

A 2005 survey by the Conference Board showed job satisfaction at an all-time low, with about 14 percent of the total number of respondents reporting that they were very satisfied with their jobs. Of the five thousand households interviewed, only one out of every three workers was satisfied with his or her pay. Only one out of every five workers was satisfied with the opportunity for advancement.[6] So why do people choose work they don't especially like?

One answer might be found in the results of the 2007 "Getting Paid in America" survey conducted by the American Payroll Association, which found that 67 percent of American families are only one paycheck away from financial hardship.[7] Even two-income families, which might be better off, would have to significantly cut back on their lifestyles if one income ended. The heads of such households don't want to risk deprivation.

Of course, this isn't new. People have long traded satisfaction for security. In his book *Working*, written nearly three decades ago, Studs Terkel observes, "Most people's jobs are too small for their spirits."[8] For security, at one time or another most of us have settled for what we had: a job, a relationship, or something else that "happened" to us that we didn't relish.

In fact, job security is an illusion. We have been brought up to believe we can survive on a single source of income. In the 1950s, common wisdom about how to have a successful career borrowed a page from the Japanese: find the right company, such as IBM, follow the rules, and you'll have security for life. Yet we know this is no longer true. Companies get downsized, philosophies of management change, and even entire organizations become obsolete. Courts have allowed some companies that filed bankruptcy to do away with pensions earned over decades.

Do you relate to any of these statistics? If you associate work predominantly with the need to create cash flow so you can pay your bills and support your lifestyle, perhaps you, like most people, have forgotten that you have a choice about what you do. Perhaps you have chosen to stay in your current job not because you love it but because it's familiar and meets your financial needs. Even though you probably enjoy aspects of what you do, you might gladly trade it in for another, more satisfying and lucrative occupation. Any sense of restlessness is a sign that your soul is ready to grow.

Answering the call of your soul by pursuing a new entrepreneurial activity or a form of creative expression, such as writing, playing music, or sculpting, would be a natural process in aligning yourself with Spirit. If you are restless, this is how you are being guided or invited by your soul to find deeper fulfillment through more satisfying work and meaningful service.

The following story is an example of the transformation that opening to the flow of soul currency can bring to anyone's life, including yours.

MYRNA'S STORY

For Myrna Miott Woods, an African American woman in her late thirties, the biggest problem was finding a way to be of service to others and still be able to pay her bills. It was the same issue she'd dealt with throughout her career.

As a college student at Drexel University, in Pennsylvania, she had volunteered for the Mayor's Commission on Literacy and a nonprofit group called Women Organized Against Rape. She found she had a heartfelt connection with her community, so after graduating she took a job as an elementary schoolteacher in Dade County, Florida. It was fun and she liked the children, but it didn't pay very well.

Myrna always seemed to gravitate to computers. During

school she had worked in the computer science department, and after she moved to Florida following graduation she mainly used email to keep in touch with her friends back home. One day when she stopped by a travel agency to buy a train ticket, she saw that the agency had a side business building websites for travel agents, physicians, dentists, and other businesspeople. She was fascinated by what they were doing. They offered to train her to do Internet marketing if she would give them a few hours of her time every week, working for a modest wage in their shop after school hours.

Myrna felt that, at the very least, it would be a way to bring in a little extra cash while having fun playing around on the computer. Since she counted on every last penny of her schoolteacher's salary to cover her monthly expenses, she needed a part-time job to make ends meet. Little did Myrna realize that this "chance" encounter in the travel agency in 1997 would eventually land her a well-paying job at R. H. Donnelly, a large marketing company.

Two years after Myrna took the job with the travel agency, in the midst of the dot-com technology boom, R. H. Donnelly hired her and she received a pay increase that meant she no longer needed to work two jobs. But now, as Myrna sat in her office at a company where her responsibility was to maintain the computer network and expand the company's website and support, she wondered if she had made a mistake in giving up her teaching job for a job that provided more money. As she looked at the walls of her office, she thought about how much she missed having contact with a community like the one that had surrounded her at the school.

The answer to Myrna's question — which one was more important to her, money or meaning? — came unexpectedly several months later when R. H. Donnelly decided to sell its stake in the fledgling Internet division. The announcement, made the day after Thanksgiving, came as an enormous shock to most of the employees in the Internet division, since it meant they no longer had jobs. Myrna was one of the few employees in that division retained to ease the transition. The job would simply provide her a paycheck for several more weeks, until the final day of her employment.

Was this an opportunity to go where her heart wanted to go? If so, where would this be? She remembered what a financial struggle teaching had been. Perhaps she could work in a nonprofit organization and use her experience in computers and web design. She floated her résumé to her friends and to headhunters in the hopes that they would know of an organization that could use her.

Myrna did not have long to wait. A local headhunter connected her to Food for the Poor, a large, multi-billion-dollar charity headquartered nearby. Myrna was needlessly nervous as she drove to the interview. She was met by a smiling woman who immediately put her at ease and told her how impressed she was with Myrna's background. As they talked, they discovered a synchronicity between them: they had the same birthday.

Myrna began serving as the charity's web designer and webmaster and designed an attractive and inviting website. When the charity sought to increase its donations, in 2002 Myrna made improvements to the existing website, applying marketing and information-architecture principles. Her team organized several Internet campaigns. In 2005, they launched a new site. Six years after starting work for the charity, and after generating more than $8 million in funds for it, Myrna became known as one of the nonprofit industry's experts on online fundraising.

Her job enabled her to serve as a local and online community liaison, and to apply her programming and other computer skills to marketing, something that had always fascinated her. She became one of the charity's highest paid employees. Myrna still put in a lot of hours, but the hours didn't seem long, because she had a sense of purpose and satisfaction in her work. As she used her skills to reach online donors, she knew that each dollar raised might make the difference between a family going hungry or learning to become self-sufficient.

Myrna recently left Food for the Poor to become a principal in a consulting firm that advises nonprofit organizations, including charities and churches, on how to do comparable online campaigns. As she told me, "Over the years my focus has changed from striving to survive (which at times was changed to striving to get rich) to striving to build the kingdom of God by serving others." Myrna is a master of soul currency.

SPIRITUAL INTELLIGENCE

In recent articles and books, many psychologists and researchers have chosen to define our use of the inner qualities of being as new forms of intelligence. Noted psychologist Howard Gardner, author of *Frames of Mind*, is credited as being the first to coin the phrase *emotional intelligence*, a term later made popular by Daniel Goleman in his bestselling book *Emotional Intelligence*. Gardner also developed the theory of "multiple intelligences" to describe various kinds of inner talents that each of us brings to life.

Neurologist Danah Zohar and physicist Ian Marshall coauthored the groundbreaking book *Spiritual Capital*, which discusses the power of using spiritual values to develop a new model of the corporation. They define *spiritual intelligence* as the manner in which we use our ethics and the different talents that characterize our beings so we may prosper.

Becoming a master of soul currency also requires us to develop a special kind of intelligence so we may bridge the material and spiritual worlds. Ultimately, whether we borrow concepts from the fields of physics, psychology, or finance, we are still referring to the same thing: the organizing power of Spirit creatively flowing through a human being. Emotional and spiritual intelligence, and the multiplicity of talents we all possess to whatever degree, are elements of our soul currency.

As I mentioned in the introduction, in this book I am using terms such as *assets, capital, currency,* and the like to talk about more powerful aspects of intelligence that exist in the invisible universe. For example, musical talent is a form of intelligence that is also a spiritual asset. From an economic perspective, we can invest this asset by a process of loving intention and thus use it to engage in capital formation, drawing both tangible returns, such as income or improved relationships, and intangible returns, such as joy and satisfaction.

Spiritual capital, the ultimate renewable resource, multiplies and grows stronger with use and intention. Learning to recognize when, why, and how to invest our spiritual capital to produce great abundance is a lesson the soul teaches. With practice, we become smarter and more efficient investors.

THE IMPORTANCE OF RECEIVING

Most people have no trouble giving. When they do hesitate, it's usually because of a perceived limitation of resources and because of ignorance about the law of circulation, which says that what is given returns to the giver magnified. It's human nature to express compassion. Even small children instinctively reach over to help someone in need, an altruistic phenomenon that many researchers now believe is part of our genetic code. Giving freely both feels good and reminds us of our true nature. But it's often easier to give to others than to ourselves.

The Bible teaches that "it is more blessed to give than to receive." However, to live fully in the flow of the soul's currency, you must do both. If you believe yourself to be a separate being, then loving yourself and even being open to receiving good from others might appear to be an exercise in narcissism, a temptation that promises to lead you down a path to excessive self-involvement, or a sin.

The great Buddha gave us another perspective: "You can search throughout the entire universe for someone who is more deserving of your love and affection than you are yourself, and that person is not to be found anywhere. You, yourself, as much as anybody in the entire universe, deserve your love and affection."[9] After all, we are created in the energy image of the Creator, with a treasure chest of divine gifts. What within us would be unlovable?

Most of us, as we conduct our everyday lives, exhibit difficulty in receiving. I have heard several people over the years announce with great pride that they treat their pets better than they treat themselves. We sometimes mistakenly view love as the denial of the self, and therefore we too often subordinate our needs to those of loved ones and friends. We spend our time working for and donating money to "worthy causes" even when our finances are out of order.

Don't mistake my message. There's nothing wrong with giving to loved ones, friends, and charities. Every opportunity to give is a chance to reveal love and open up the heart. But when the circulation of love is stopped by an inability to receive, then eventually we have little or nothing to give.

If you have trouble receiving in your own life, you may have come up with a wonderfully clever way to disguise your inability, which is to become extra generous with your time, attention, talents, and money. This is a common means of concealing the truth, especially among people who are self-identified as "spiritual." But in situations where circulation is impeded, the outward flow of love eventually dwindles to a trickle.

If you have ever wondered why seemingly unspiritual people can come from nothing and end up multimillionaires, while seemingly spiritual people struggle to earn money, you must first accept that all of us are spiritual beings connected to the flow of soul currency. One of the major reasons people are able to cultivate affluence is that prosperous people have opened themselves up to receive. Most highly prosperous people don't question whether they deserve money, real estate, and tangible assets. In fact, they believe they deserve an abundant cash flow. In areas of their lives not represented on a balance sheet, such as relationships and joyfulness, they may be less receptive. We can never presume to know what's going on in someone's life, unless that person is a close friend who confides all his or her thoughts and feelings to us.

My experience is that enlightened millionaires understand the circular flow of soul currency and are prosperous in every area of their lives — or are moving toward personal as well as material abundance. These individuals are so receptive that their love overflows and gives back to the world. Their enterprises employ, sustain, and involve scores of other people besides themselves.

I encourage you to begin, from this day forward, to value yourself more fully by consciously looking for new ways to love yourself and by being open to receive the gifts you are given. By loving yourself and expressing gratitude for what is present, you affirm your connection to others and the universe. In connection, there is flow. So, in addition, keep noticing where you are connected.

The infinite intelligence is always prompting us to become

more than we are and to open up to love. Our souls are always nudging us to love ourselves and to recognize, in each moment, how to express Spirit. Part of the secret of the journey is to be able to live in the mystery. The urgency within us is so insistent that we often cocreate circumstances where the need to love ourselves becomes too loud to ignore.

If you're not feeling as prosperous as you'd like to be, remember that prosperity and love are integrated. You can walk through either doorway and end up in the same room. Your discomfort could be your spiritual wake-up call. For some people it's easier to understand love than money, so they seek to connect with love. In most cases, people find it easier to start with the outward symbols of prosperity, and then learn to work with spiritual equivalents of those symbols, only in the process discovering love.

THE POWER OF ENTERPRISE

We've got our mastery of the material world partially right. Many of us agree about the value of items such as real estate, blue-chip stocks, triple-A-rated bonds, and precious metals and gemstones. But when they are not invested, or utilized, assets become static, lifeless, and hold value only on paper. Under certain conditions, such as when a company is awarded a large customer contract, hires a new chief executive officer, or gets a property rezoned so more buildings can be built, the value of the company's stock or real estate holdings go up.

Since, as science is beginning to discover, we are creating our world from within ourselves, this begs the question: where can each of us measure the value that we personally add to everything we do? Most people highly value what they can see. Wouldn't true value be derived from our investments of our spiritual assets? Development of our spiritual assets adds value to our expression of

Spirit. Isn't it spiritual intelligence, which I spoke of earlier in the chapter, that enables us to make wise investments?

When intention and the energy of love are focused on spiritual assets, this transforms them into a powerful form of capital, which has an exponential growth potential when invested in a specific enterprise. Spiritual capital comes alive when we invest love in attaining a particular goal.

It is overly simplistic to think of someone who utilizes his or her inner spiritual gifts as being conscious and loving at all times. But the very process of learning to be aware of our true nature often entails experiencing what appears to be the opposite. One female student of mine, for example, who had been molested as a child, experienced powerful distrust and extreme irritability whenever she worked for a male client. This kind of obstacle is part of the journey we take while developing consciousness, which often requires us to come to terms with our childhood wounds and transform our limiting and intolerant beliefs. Eventually, we may recognize that all is one, and that our most fulfilling experiences are those in which we are loved or give love.

In a conversation on PBS with journalist Bill Moyers, which was later published as a book, *The Power of Myth*, Joseph Campbell said of the spiritual intelligence guiding us: "If you do follow your bliss, you put yourself on a kind of track that has been there all the while, waiting for you, and the life that you ought to be living is the one you are living. . . . I say, follow your bliss and don't be afraid, and doors will open where you didn't know they were going to be."[10]

We use soul currency in our relationships, in corporate boardrooms, and in creative endeavors. What we achieve with our soul currency is highly valued, even prized. It's ironic, therefore, that we often take for granted or sweep aside the tools of Spirit. We tend to look for material cause-and-effect explanations instead.

If you are reading this book, it's likely that you are the type of person who has made the gradual shift from an unconscious, separated life to a more spiritual metaphysical awareness of your connection with all of life, and are engaged in the creativity that this connected life virtually insists upon.

MASTERING SOUL CURRENCY

The next five chapters of *Soul Currency* will guide you through a process of incorporating in your life the vast and powerful world of your inner, spiritual resources. The strongest underlying thought that can prevent you from living a prosperous, fulfilled life is the belief that you are not deserving or worthy enough. The steps you'll take are designed to heal such a belief.

Love and forgiveness for both yourself and others is the prerequisite for fulfilled living and prosperity. You are constantly in the flow of energy. Any thoughts of fear, resentment, anger, vengefulness, or unworthiness repel the very energy that circulates goodness. In the presence of such thoughts, the energy of creative flow takes a detour and moves around you instead of through you.

The person who exemplifies being outside the flow of soul currency is one who always has many possibilities but sees few if any come through. Or this person may be one who feels stuck in a situation or faces constant delays.

We are the vehicles through which soul currency operates, and we are its very essence. Through our choices and intentions — our enterprises — we join with this energy in the infinite continuum that flows throughout all eternity, returning to the source. The key to becoming a master of the material world is to become aware of how the energy of creation simultaneously flows through us and *is* us.

Being a master of soul currency means that you have mastered the ability to listen to the spiritual side of yourself that is your connection to the Divine. (No, this doesn't necessarily mean that God will tell you to quit your job, move to a remote region of the country, and start an animal rights project, although if you would love to do these things you certainly are free to choose them.) Spirit gives you choices, including the choice to be happy, prosperous, and fulfilled doing what you already love in your daily life. You can learn to live in the flow of soul currency.

EXERCISES FOR YOUR SOUL

Here and in subsequent chapters, you'll find sets of exercises designed to help you encourage the circulation of soul currency in your life. These include sequences of activities that reveal equivalencies between the material world of money and Spirit; opportunities to practice boosting the flow of soul currency in your personal life; and powerful meditations.

MANAGING YOUR SPIRITUAL PORTFOLIO

Follow the Flow of Currency

Currency has often been described as the lifeblood of commerce permeating all cultures. For instance, a U.S. dollar can be exchanged for hundreds of other currencies, which, as we have seen, are symbols of value by agreement. The symbol of currency is just the tip of the iceberg of flow and creative value. Currency shape-shifts into other forms, tangible and intangible. Looking at your own life, list five visible and five intangible forms currency takes.

My tangible currency includes (examples: cash, stocks, real estate, and collectibles):

1.

2.

3.

4.

5.

My intangible currency includes (examples: education, vocational training, service):

1.

2.

3.

4.

5.

PERSONAL EXPERIENCE

Build a Better Belief System

You might say that soul currency is a form of divinely inspired purchasing power, because it helps us create what we want. In a world created from the inside out, the creative process begins with thoughts, which are molded by heart-centered consciousness. What internal beliefs would you choose in order to open the flow of four different aspects of your soul currency?

Financial prosperity: "I choose to believe..."
Social connections: "I choose to believe..."
Intellectual inspiration: "I choose to believe..."
Spiritual awareness: "I choose to believe..."

MEDITATION

Create a Harmonious Life

Sit quietly in a comfortable position. Close your eyes and breathe easily. As you enter a calm, meditative state, envision yourself seated at the center of a six-pointed star that represents the unity of six primary aspects of your life: health, relationships, work, money, spirituality, and home. Each point of the star signifies one of these aspects.

Imagine filling the star with the energy of universal light. Concentrate first on filling up the area around your solar plexus, then allow the light to saturate each cell in your body and expand to fill your entire energy field, until there is light surrounding you. Rest in this light-filled energy field for two minutes. Finish the meditation by pulling the entire six-pointed star and its energy into your heart.

SPIRITUAL ASSETS

2 | Recognizing the Real Value of Your Inner Treasure

What lies behind us and what lies before us are tiny matters compared to what lies within us.

— AUTHOR UNKNOWN

If your goal is to earn a living by doing something that delights you and serves others, the first step in your soul currency program is to take an inventory of your spiritual assets and make an honest assessment of them. Without recognizing that you possess these positive inner qualities, natural abilities, and divine gifts, you cannot develop the ability to leverage or magnify them to create a prosperous flow of loving energy in your life. Your spiritual assets, which seem invisible to the naked eye, have a depth of being and a richness of possibility greater than any material assets, such as stocks, real estate, and gold. From a metaphysical perspective, your spiritual assets are more real than anything you could ever touch or hold in your hands. Your creative passion and feelings of purpose and fulfillment all emanate from the essential "be-ingness" of your spiritual assets.

Spiritual assets are universal, and they are unlimited in scope.

Anyone who recognizes and embraces his or her own spiritual assets can effectively access their power. For example, Thomas Alva Edison used intuition and imagination to design the electric lightbulb and many other inventions. James Watt used these same two spiritual assets to design the steam engine. Later on, Gordon Moore, founder of Intel, used them to innovate microprocessors. Spiritual assets are an open energy field of possibilities, or a "divine imprint" of the Creator, that you and every person on earth are endowed with in some measure.

Capitalizing on your spiritual assets requires more than developing a simple awareness of them, however. After you recognize your spiritual assets, you must embrace and incorporate their "aliveness," power, and value in everything you do. You have the ability to shape your world creatively through your clarity of intention and the choices you make. Your spiritual assets have great value only because you use them in meaningful ways that build value and contribute to the world.

Often people take spiritual assets for granted. Even the assets they appreciate, they tend to undervalue. You fall into this category if you're aware of your potential and yet have learned to live as if you had no part in creating your life. Do you tend to focus on what you don't have, rather than on what's inside you waiting to emerge? Do you judge yourself harshly when you "screw up," and almost never pat yourself on the back for the hundreds of little things you do right each day? Do you have moments when you wonder if you're good enough to deserve success and love? If so, then the first step in the soul currency program is especially important for you.

Almost everyone has heard some version of the story by Russell Conwell, a motivational speaker and founder of Temple University in Philadelphia, about the South Asian farmer who ignorantly tossed aside many of the black stones he encountered in the soil on his property as he scratched out a living.[1] After many years, he finally sold his farm in order to seek his fortune elsewhere. Little did he know that the black stones that peppered his fields and streambeds, and that he had considered a nuisance, were actually raw diamonds. These acres of diamonds ultimately became the famous Golconda Diamond Mine, one of the richest mines ever and the producer of such crown jewels as the stunning Kohinoor diamond of England and the fabulous Orlov diamond of Russia.

"If only he'd been more observant, he'd have become wildly wealthy" may have been your first reaction to this tale. Indeed, that's the lesson for everyone. Look carefully. You have your own acres of diamonds within you. Your spiritual assets are legion. Like the farmer with the black stones, you may be paying more attention to the superficial appearance of what your life holds than to the truth that you have everything within you necessary to create wealth, happiness, fulfilling relationships, and more.

For too long, you may have believed you are "stuck with the cards that God dealt you." Using the same analogy, if you've peeked at two or three cards in the deck and believe that someone else got all the valuable cards, it's time to look again.

EXPERIENCING VALUE THROUGH LOSS:
THE EBAY GAME

On the first day of my abundance course, I have participants play a game designed to help them recognize the value of their spiritual assets. They begin by dividing into small groups and devising a list of spiritual assets that fall into four categories: intuition and guidance, creativity, higher personality traits, and cultivated skills and knowledge (see table 1). From this master list, participants are instructed to select one of their least-utilized assets, which they then pretend to auction off on eBay. I ask them to imagine that this means they won't be able to use this asset themselves for a period of twenty years following the sale.

TABLE 1

Partial List of Spiritual Assets

INTUITION AND GUIDANCE

Clairaudience
Clairsentience
Clairvoyance
Faith in outcome
Faith in self
Faith in spirit
Insight
Inspiration
Intelligence
Intention
Purpose
Wisdom

HIGHER PERSONALITY
TRAITS

Consideration
Discernment
Empathy
Generosity
Harmony
Joyfulness
Kindness
Optimism
Persistence
Reason
Selflessness

CREATIVITY

Ability to dream at night
Ability to speak a foreign
    language
Ability to use color well
Ability to write
Artistic ability
Dexterity
Good spatial relations
Humor
Imagination
Mathematical ability
Musical ability
Perception

CULTIVATED SKILLS
AND KNOWLEDGE

Avocational interests
Career training
Facility with language
Friendship and social
    skills
Good physical condition
Knowledge of culture
Knowledge of history
Knowledge of
    mathematics
Networking skills

Even though it's an imaginary auction, this exercise usually causes quite a stir among my students, because being forced to sell one of their assets on the spot (and explain why they should get the best price possible for it) suddenly causes them to consider how much it's really worth. Almost every person who undertakes this exercise has difficulty choosing which asset to sell. Nearly all my students realize that even their most undervalued asset *could* be of far more value to them if they remembered it more often. Some anguish so much over their selections that they have to be reminded that this is just an exercise. Only when they experience the feeling of loss stimulated by the exercise do they begin to appreciate the value of their own assets.

After the students select an asset to sell, I ask them to assign a price. Frequently, when it comes to putting a value on the asset they've selected, they tell me the asset is "priceless." I remind them that everything has a price. However high it is, it's what a willing seller would take from a willing buyer. Yes, these assets are potentially priceless, but it's only through use that they truly have value for us.

Ironically, because the value some students place on their assets is so great, the enormous price has no real meaning to them. Many students are inclined to start valuing their assets in the billions. So I remind them of what $1 billion could buy. For example, Trump Tower in New York City has a value of around $300 million. An F-15 fighter plane goes for $16 million (one was actually offered for sale on eBay). The net value of the Harry Potter brand has been estimated by Wall Street to be around $1 billion. Put another way, $1 billion could feed most of the starving children in West Africa for half a decade.[2] This figure is larger than the entire economies of most underdeveloped countries.

When students claim such a high value, it indicates they have little or no emotional connection to the answer. The huge number reflects how they see their inner value. Rather than meaning that their sense of inner value is extraordinarily high, it signifies that their value is an "intellectual" value and not heartfelt. Frequently, the higher the value for the asset, the lower the self-worth.

I started putting a limit on the price people could ask for each spiritual asset during the game when it became evident that the people who had the most trouble with prosperity were the ones who came up with numbers like a "gazillion." One perpetually out-of-work computer programmer actually came up with a price tag of a googol dollars (a one followed by a hundred zeros), which was an amount far beyond his reality.

As the next step in our game, participants are directed to write a sparkling eBay advertisement with an eye-catching headline. I provide them with a personal financial balance sheet that includes a special formula and line for valuing "spiritual assets." By multiplying the remaining assets on the partial list (about forty of them; see table 1, page 40) by the price of the asset they propose to sell on eBay, they can arrive at a conservative estimated value. Then, after they fill in the rest of the balance sheet, the last thing they do is calculate their net worth by subtracting their liabilities from their assets (see table 2, which shows the numbers one participant came up with).

The results of the game are eye-popping for my students. Nearly all of them have an individual net worth that ranges from hundreds of millions to billions of dollars. Of course, fully 99.5 percent of the value shown on those balance sheets is composed of people's spiritual assets, demonstrating both the qualitative value and the enormous potential that each person has within. I've included a blank balance sheet in the appendix of this book (page 225), and I encourage you to spend some time filling it out and experiencing the results for yourself.

TABLE 2

Personal Financial Balance Sheet

ASSETS		LIABILITIES	
CURRENT ASSETS		CURRENT LIABILITIES	
Cash and equivalents	$6,345	Payables	$3,230
Stocks, bonds, and securities	$5,800	Short-term debt (under one year)	$16,400
Short-term receivables	$0	SUBTOTAL CURRENT	
Other	$400	LIABILITIES	$19,630
SUBTOTAL CURRENT ASSETS	$12,545		
OTHER ASSETS		OTHER LIABILITIES	
Real estate	$289,000	Bank debt (over one year)	$14,900
Other investments (nonliquid)	$4,000	Notes	$225,000
Personal effects	$17,800	Contingent liabilities	$0
Equipment (including auto) and fixtures	$6,900	SUBTOTAL OTHER LIABILITIES	$239,900
Collectibles, art, and so on	$2,000		
SUBTOTAL OTHER ASSETS	$319,700	TOTAL LIABILITIES	$259,530
SUBTOTAL SPIRITUAL ASSETS (from exercise)	$140,500,000	NET WORTH*	$140,572,715
		TOTAL LIABILITIES	
TOTAL ASSETS	$140,832,245	+ NET WORTH	$140,832,245

% Tangible assets**/total assets ($332,245/$140,832,245)	0.24%
(What percentage of your total assets are your tangible assets?)	
% Spiritual assets/total assets ($140,500,000/$140,832,245)	99.76%
(What percentage of your total assets are your spiritual assets?)	

* Net worth = total assets – total liabilities
** Tangible assets = subtotal current assets + subtotal other assets

LOVE: THE POWER BEHIND
YOUR SPIRITUAL ASSETS

As I discussed in the introduction and chapter 1, the energy of love that infuses each of our beings is the essence of Spirit. Love is experienced as many different feelings, from deep caring for another person to altruism, well-being, kindness, and empathy. People generally mistake these loving feelings for the essence of the energy of love itself, when in fact love not only underlies our feelings but is also continually shape-shifting, taking nearly an infinite number of other forms in our lives. People mistake love for a personal experience, when it really is universal creative energy.

To say love itself is a spiritual asset would be like saying that gravity is an asset. Rather, it is an underlying force in our lives. Our spiritual assets are forms of love, like members of a grand orchestra whose purpose is to interpret Spirit's essence. The way we use these assets and the beliefs we have about them give us a sense of "personalness." Because these assets seem to be coming from us as individuals, we often fail to realize they are, in fact, part of the universal energy.

THE FOUR TYPES OF SPIRITUAL ASSETS

Let's take a look at the four categories of spiritual assets. Remember that they are always working in combination at any given moment, and it's always your choice whether to use them. Some you probably use so naturally and automatically that, until now, you've been unconscious of how you incorporate them in your life. No wonder spiritual assets tend to be undervalued resources. (In chapter 3, I discuss the great activators of spiritual assets: thought and intention.)

Intuition and Guidance as Spiritual Assets

Many of the most successful people in the world, including government leaders and the chief executives of major corporations, rely upon intuition and guidance to help them make important decisions, assess colleagues and adversaries, and navigate business opportunities and problems. Everyone has an internal guidance system that scans beyond the boundaries of time and the material world as we know it. Recognizing and using this resource affects our choices and lives. What are these assets, and how may we define them?

Intuition is a knowing voice that originates from deep within us. We may hear this voice during meditation or contemplation, or receive messages from it through our dreams at night or while going about mundane daily activities. People experience their intuition in different ways; however, there is nearly always a sense of "rightness" about intuition, a feeling of having penetrated beyond the obvious, surface layer of the world. An unexplained insight may hold a warning, such as "If you walk down that street, you'll be putting yourself in danger," or "These people are shading the truth about the product they are selling." Later on, hunches like these often prove to be correct.

One highly successful fund manager and technology company analyst, who describes himself as "essentially a right-brained person with a left-brained vocabulary," has the ability to assess the big picture in new situations, so that his first instincts about what to do are uncannily accurate. He makes decisions based on his intuitive feelings, rather than logic, even though he works in a business that most people associate with provable facts and rationality. After first consulting his gut instinct, or intuition, he does his "homework," following through with due diligence to ensure that his initial feelings are supported.

On one occasion, this analyst evaluated a seemingly success-ful maker of ATMs that had projected rapid growth. The day before he visited the company, he dreamed that its stock would unexpectedly drop 90 percent, so instead of buying he considered whether to warn his clients, who held large amounts of the com-pany's stock.

Prompted by the image of impending disaster supplied by his intuitive dream, he kept digging and asking questions, until he discovered that a large number of the company's orders were con-ditional on delivery within a specific time frame, and there had been delays in securing key parts to complete the units. The com-pany would not be able to deliver on time, and the orders would be canceled. His dream information was accurate. Thus his in-tuition had enabled him to recommend that his clients sell their shares, whereas all other analysts had strongly recommended buying the stock.

Guidance is a message of wisdom that comes to us in some fashion from outside us, usually when we are lost or don't feel entirely clear about what we're doing. Like intuition, guidance comes in many forms, including synchronicity, which has been defined as a coincidence that holds meaning for the person ex-periencing it. Guidance often puts someone in the right place at the right time to receive a message, such as when he or she happens to hear a snippet of an interview on the car radio that supplies exactly the information needed, or to see a timely arti-cle in a magazine at a supermarket checkout counter, or to sit next to someone on an airplane who supplies precisely the information he or she needs to hear.

People sometimes dismiss coincidences like these as "fortu-nate accidents," when in fact the soul's greater guidance system is not limited to information but includes chance encounters. Al-though these phenomena defy logic, they are widely recognized as real. By pointing to the presence of an underlying pattern in our lives and everything around us, these spiritual assets affirm our connection to the infinite intelligence of the universe.

Quantum physicist Amit Goswami, who describes himself as a consciousness scientist, has often asserted that the universe is self-aware, and that what we recognize as material reality is literally created by consciousness. Guidance and intuition open the way for us to be successful, abundant, and happy: as the soul's navigation devices, they show us the best direction to take at a given moment. People who follow through on the messages they receive, such as the woman in the next story, serve as living proof of their potential significance.

In late 1995, Deborah Weidenhamer was traveling almost non-stop, commuting between her home in Phoenix and her office in San Francisco, where she worked as a mergers and acquisitions consultant, as well as crisscrossing the country to visit clients. On one flight home, she used frequent flyer miles for an upgrade to first class, where she expected to relax, recover from an intense week, and get a little sleep. Instead she found herself seated next to a grizzled old auctioneer.

"How perfect," she thought. "So much for getting any rest." She found herself entertained by the man's stories and fascinated by what she perceived to be a lucrative and exciting life. When she got home, she immediately started to do some research. She found that the auction industry was fragmented, made up of small local auction companies run by auctioneers like the man she'd met on the plane.

What if companies could be run professionally, have adequate capital, and astutely market themselves? Deborah recognized that meeting the old auctioneer had given her an incredible opportunity. The auction industry had greater sales than the largest retail stores put together! One of the most challenging things she would have to do would be to take the first step: go to auctioneer school to learn to speak the rapid-fire auctioneer lingo. Deborah began working out of her garage, alone. She started looking into niche markets, such as government contracts to sell road equipment and property confiscated from drug dealers. She had a successful first year with $160,000 in sales. Now in her thirteenth year, she employs more than fifty people, not counting auctioneers. She had sales in 2007 of nearly $38 million, and business was so robust due to the recession that she was forced to turn away business.

What has propelled the company is Deborah's insight that she could use the Internet to simulcast auctions so that buyers could come from anywhere. Rather than fighting eBay and other consumer auction sites that might compete, as the industry tried to do, she saw an opportunity to join them — but on a private world stage.

The daughter of a minister who was also an entrepreneur, Deborah sees business as a spiritual path. She prays daily for guidance and recognizes opportunities, such as meeting the auctioneer on the plane, as blessings. She sees herself as a good businesswoman, and she manages the company with a vision that encompasses more than simply the bottom line.[3]

Besides "chance" meetings such as the one Deb Weidenhamer experienced, there are many other ways the universe provides guidance. Our intuition, which reaches beyond our five senses, is always offering guidance when we tune in to it. Psychics are so enormously sensitive to guidance that they demonstrate special gifts that go beyond the usual perceptions of the five senses. Yet even if we don't consider ourselves to be psychic, we all have these gifts to some degrees. Clairaudience is the psychic ability to hear spiritual voices that may not be audible to anyone else and to receive intuitive information in the form of spoken words. Clairsentience is the psychic ability to feel the presence of spirits, and simply to know what's happening around you out of sight. Clairvoyance is the psychic ability to envision pictures, symbolic images, or events not perceived by the eyes or other senses.

Allow yourself to reflect for a moment on occasions when you've been guided and the role that intuition plays in your life. Have you ever had an experience of extrasensory perception, received a message in a dream, or suddenly felt clear about how to successfully manage a complicated situation in your life, or clear about the underlying details of a business deal that lacked actual transparency? Is this strong? Is it weak? Do you trust it?

The trick in developing spiritual assets is to learn to listen to the voice of intuition and take it seriously. One of my mentors and friends, the late Jay Wells, founder of Wells National Services, was highly skilled at this kind of discernment, and it brought him great abundance. He received such a message when he was hospitalized for an ailment in the late 1950s. Never one to sit still, even in a hospital bed, he noticed there were no televisions available for bedridden patients. Having had a part interest in a hotel that had introduced televisions in every room, he asked why patients couldn't watch TV. "That's the way it is," he was informed. "Maybe someone should do something about it."

Wells told me that he perceived this comment as a message meant especially for him. Always the entrepreneur, he was tantalized by the prospect of putting TVs into tens of thousands of hospital rooms in New York City alone, as well as in the hundreds of thousands of hospital rooms across the country. Like hotel guests, patients could choose to rent a TV, and watching it would give them something to do while they endured forced bed rest. Subsequently, Wells National Services, which pioneered the installation of pay televisions in hospitals, became the leader in the field and eventually was bought out by the corporate giant American Home Products.

As you begin to open to and trust your intuition and actively seek to receive messages from Spirit, you'll notice that your guidance becomes stronger and clearer.

Creativity as a Spiritual Asset

Creativity in its many forms is one of the greatest assets of the soul. Like your other spiritual assets, it is infused with love, the essence of creation. When you feel inspired by ideas that just come, you are swept up in Spirit's creative flow, your imagination is stimulated, and you express yourself in myriad ways, from writing to music to humor, or you may even find yourself doing a routine task differently. Spiritual assets in this category are activated when you are swept up in the beat of music and express it through dance, or when your imagination comes to life and you are swept away by stories, or when you feel frustrated that the world is not perfect and you divine a new way to change it for the better.

When I was a student at Amherst College, often I was visited by Walter Simonson, one of my friends across the hall in our dorm. An affable, bespectacled geology major, Walt always seemed serious to people who didn't know him. His parents wanted him to study medicine, but Walt had another side to him. He loved to draw fantasy stories, especially about superheroes such as Spider-Man and the Fantastic Four. On Saturday nights, he would show me the carefully crafted original episodes that were as good as or better than anything Marvel Comics was then publishing.

Walt eventually began developing his own superheroes, and his Saturday night presentations became increasingly more elaborate, complete with the usual sound effects: "Boom!" "Kazow!" "Pow!" I would find myself caught up in a parallel universe, unfettered by the so-called mature idea that future geologists and journalists should not so fervently enjoy superhero comics. Occasionally, as I weighed my own prospects as a history major, I found myself wondering if Mr. and Mrs. Simonson ever despaired about what Walt would do for a living. If so, they needn't have worried.

Today Walt Simonson is one of this country's most beloved comic book writers and illustrators. His versatility, joy, and talent show in the large body of work he has done, from illustrations for *The Hobbit* and a detective series in the 1970s, to the Marvel Comics classics produced in the 1980s and 1990s, such as *Thor* and *X-Factor* (the latter being a collaboration with his wife, Louise Simonson), to *Elric: The Making of a Sorcerer*, an illustrated novel written by Michael Moorcock. Walt has been honored with many awards and has reached the top of his profession. His signature is his last name distorted to resemble a dinosaur.

As Walt's success proves, you can be well paid to do what you love. You are at your most powerful when you follow your creative passion and let it inspire your choices and your path. Creativity is the spiritual asset that gives you the ability to imagine and respond to the great flow of life. When you let your creative energies flow, you become a shining channel for Spirit. You will often be amazed at what flows out of you.

This capacity underlies many different kinds of creative gifts, which include inborn talents for music, drawing, inventing, and movement, to name only a few. Change in our lives is inevitable, as the universe is always shifting. Our creativity allows us to evolve, adapt, and transform, and what arises is often more expansive than what it replaces. Our inner fountain of creative genius enables us to sense ourselves as alive and in motion.

All of us, whether or not we acknowledge it, have a set of creative gifts — whether for creating fine art, making music, bringing people together, decorating with colors, cooking gourmet meals, solving numerical equations, playing or designing computer games, cultivating friendships, or something else. What makes these spiritual assets so special is that their expression is as unique as the individuals who possess them.

For a moment, allow yourself to reflect on your particular creative gifts. Where in your life do you feel most creative? Do you draw upon creative assets in your work? Do you reserve creativity for leisure time? Are you feeling creatively blocked or creatively fulfilled?

The joy that often ensues when you use your creative gifts is multiplied when you share them with others. By nurturing them, your creative assets become part of your destiny. You may begin a career on one path and then be led down another path by your soul's connection to your creative gifts. One of my friends and students, Nicolas Villamizar, discovered this.

Nicolas, a native of Venezuela, has had a love affair with all aspects of the music business since childhood. His family insisted that he study civil engineering, so it wasn't until he graduated from college in his native country that he pursued his true passion, music. He was accepted at, and later graduated from, the Berklee College of Music in Boston, and then received a master's degree from the New England Conservatory. After graduation, he found himself playing and singing weeknights at a piano bar near Cambridge, Massachusetts, but it was clear to him that he needed to find some way to supplement his income.

Nicolas's outgoing personality and his original songs endeared him to regulars at the bar, some of whom worked at the regional sales office of the minicomputer giant Digital Equipment Corporation. "Would you be able to compose a three- or four-minute song for a trade show?" one of the salespeople asked him. Wondering if this was just idle conversation, Nicolas nonetheless sent his material to the regional sales manager. He was retained a week later.

Eventually it was decided that Nicolas's three-minute song would be used as the theme song for a nationwide product launch. By employing his spiritual asset of creativity and making a commitment to pursue his passion for music, in only a few brief moments Nicolas was able to generate income equivalent to what he would normally earn for nearly a year's worth of performances.

Creativity is present nearly everywhere and in nearly anything we do. It's in the presentations you make when you "sell" yourself to others, such as during a job interview or in a business proposal. It's in the clothes you wear when you dress up for a date or a family function. It's in the photographs you take when you go on vacation.

Watch children at play. For them, a cardboard box becomes a castle, dolls become part of the family, and video games allow them to save the universe. Like children, we constantly use creativity to invent our world.

Making people laugh is an example of a creative gift that is always expressed in an individual manner. For example, contrast the silent humor of Raymond Teller of the popular comedy team Penn and Teller with the comedic genius of actor Nathan Lane or the dark, sarcastic wit of Steven Wright. These funny men have very different styles of humor. So do you and I. Creativity is one of the reasons our lives are unique.

We also use creativity when we seek to be persuasive. A mother's imaginative coaxing to persuade a recalcitrant child to eat broccoli is creative. A politician trying to convince his or her peers to vote for a needed project is creative.

As you pursue work and other activities that involve your

creative gifts, your satisfaction in what you are doing will increase. It requires less effort to do what you love than something you hate or feel merely so-so about. Once your creativity is ignited, new opportunities will emerge from the path you've created.

Higher Personality Traits as Spiritual Assets

Sometimes called character traits, the higher personality traits stem from our personal values and are fundamental in achieving success in any endeavor. These spiritual assets include optimism, the ability to focus, persistence, honesty, courage, authenticity, industriousness, and many additional qualities.

Dr. Martin Seligman is a pioneer in the field of positive psychology, which studies the empowering aspects of the emotions and psyche. In his book *Learned Optimism*, he explains how we benefit from adopting in all we do an attitude of flexible optimism, a perspective from which we can discern the positive aspects of all situations as well as the negative consequences of our choices. Flexible optimism gives us more freedom of choice.

Have you ever noticed as you go through life making different choices that reality mirrors what you believe? This goes for negative beliefs, such as "I'm not good enough to...," as well as positive beliefs, such as "Given time, I can solve any problem." Chances are that a person holding the first belief doesn't feel optimistic and is easily defeated, whereas a person holding the second belief is more likely to persevere and take necessary risks to accomplish his or her goals. We have the potential to create whatever we think and declare to be true. You might choose to understand this phenomenon as a law of quantum physics that creates reality from your beliefs, or as a loving spiritual presence that always says yes. Once you are aware of this phenomenon, you can't avoid seeing it everywhere.

Culturally, we celebrate people who demonstrate higher personality traits, such as the courageous Lance Armstrong, one of the world's best-known cancer survivors. His story of perseverance, of remaining optimistic and strong and prevailing over the testicular cancer that had reached his brain, lungs, and bones, is truly inspirational. Add to this picture his later return to world-class bicycling, and his winning the Tour de France — possibly the most grueling physical event in the world — a total of seven times in a row before his retirement.

Armstrong made me a fan of the Tour de France, which lasts twenty-three days. At first I would get up at 5 AM and watch him on the Internet, and then eventually I began watching him on one of the cable channels. I realized I was not only rooting for him to win but also wanted to be reminded of my own courage, determination, and ability to triumph over adversity, assets that often I felt could use a boost.

Armstrong's higher personality traits — his persistence, courage, and optimism, to name a few — express the quality of love and embody the power of miracles. More than 60 million people, including myself, have bought one of the simple yellow "Live Strong" rubber bracelets sold by the Lance Armstrong Foundation to remind us of our own higher qualities of courage, love, and determination, as well as to contribute funds to cancer patients and their families.

Allow yourself to reflect on your own higher personality traits. Have you ever met adversity with courage? When has your integrity been tested? Do you know how to honestly communicate difficult truths? Are you optimistic and industrious when facing a tight deadline? In celebrating the inspirational determination of a person like Lance Armstrong, do not forget that admirable qualities can also be found within you. Your task is to become aware of them and use them in life-enhancing ways.

People so often begin their enterprises with optimism and then give up on their dreams at the first sign of an obstacle. Those who develop their higher personality traits, however, have more staying power. Traits such as consideration and commitment also inspire trust between co-workers and contribute to harmony in the workplace.

Cultivated Skills and Knowledge as Spiritual Assets

You can add cultivated skills — such as those gained from a high school or college education or professional or technical training — physical conditioning, and wisdom to the list of your other spiritual assets. How such skills eventually factor into your career and success may surprise you.

Steve Jobs, the founder of Apple Computer and Pixar Animation Studios, for instance, reportedly has said that he applied skills he learned in a calligraphy course at Reed College in Portland, Oregon, in his design for the original Apple computer.[4] The computer's innovative design features enabled it to create its own market for unique products. Jobs never consciously knew that the short college course he almost didn't take would be so important to his computer design, or that Apple would become such a success.

In my own case, I always found science, especially physics and math, challenging during my school years. In high school, these subjects were the bane of my existence, whereas I shone in English and social studies. Somehow I barely made it through the required freshman college physics and math courses; how ironic that I would be invited to speak at my fifteenth college reunion about my work as the chief financial officer of a publicly held company that had made a major breakthrough in physics. No one would have predicted that my success would emerge in that area.

Once I was out of college, applying acquired math and science skills to real-life situations that I cared about and found relevant to my goals made a huge difference in my abilities. What I'd believed was a personal weakness was merely a lack of engagement with the educational materials my teachers had used. Because the work became real for me, I was motivated to transform my skill sets into a personal strength, and I was glad I'd learned them.

Among spiritual assets in this category, getting an education is primary, not only because it gives you access to valuable information but also because it teaches you how to approach learning new subjects, and how to handle circumstances when you know little or nothing about them. Education gives you tools with which to draw out the best from within you and teaches you not to fear the unknown.

One of the most worthwhile skills you can cultivate is the ability to network socially and professionally. As Keith Ferrazzi, the author of *Never Eat Lunch Alone*, says, "Connecting is one of the most important business — and life — skill sets you'll ever learn."[5] The value of a network is astronomical when it's well utilized. Depending on the number of people you know and the special abilities and knowledge each member of your network possesses, the various possibilities it provides you are nearly endless.

Of all the categories of spiritual assets, cultivated skills are perhaps the easiest ones to assign a financial value. Anyone with an accounting background can easily determine how much his or her family spent on him or her from birth to age eighteen. If you went to public school, you can determine what the taxpayers invested in you. Your family would have invested an even higher amount to pay for private school. Add to that the amount of money spent on your four years of local, state, or private college.

Take some time to consider, and perhaps jot down on paper, as many different skills as you can remember having acquired in your lifetime, from tying your shoes or baking a cake, to doing calculus or building a house, to riding a horse or dancing the mambo. You never know when a skill such as carpentry or a piece of knowledge such as the names of the planets in our solar system may come in handy.

Your unique set of skills may give you an entirely different perspective than other people. For example, Gavin Menzies, a British submarine captain, used his knowledge of the sea and a comparison of longitude and latitude markings on medieval maps to discover evidence that a Chinese fleet not only visited the Americas in 1421, more than seventy years before Columbus's expedition, but also left colonies in the Western Hemisphere. As Menzies notes in a book he published in 2003, there were three Chinese fleets, totaling more than three thousand ships. Each fleet mapped a portion of the world — and in this way the Chinese mapped the entire world. One fleet in particular mapped the Atlantic Ocean from Greenland to the Cape of Good Hope in Chile and Argentina. When Columbus reported seeing Chinese in Hispaniola, it wasn't because he'd been in the sun too long. He actually did see them, but he didn't realize that these people were part of a colony. Other historians had previously read the same information that Menzies read and had drawn different conclusions. Menzies was able to see things they had passed by because of their ignorance of maritime terminology and know-how.[6]

Cultivated skills expand your inborn talents. When employed in combination with your other spiritual assets, they are the springboards to prosperity with fulfillment.

TAKING THE NEXT STEP

As you've learned in this chapter, your spiritual assets fall into four categories — intuition and guidance, creativity, higher personality traits, and cultivated skills and knowledge — which contain the richness of possibility and the depth of your being. These are infused with love, the currency of Spirit, and it is your unique expression of love that allows you to consciously shape your destiny. An asset that enables one person to be a great entrepreneur allows another to become a great teacher, writer, or parent.

When my sudden business reversal years ago left me a million dollars in debt, it was almost natural for me to despondently affirm: "I have nothing." But then one night at a friend's house, I watched a business tycoon being interviewed on a talk show. After the talk show host recited his guest's great accomplishments, the tycoon talked about how he had turned around his life after he'd gone bankrupt. I saw a lot of similarities to my situation in his story of what turned his troubles around: he had graduated from a liberal arts college, had a background in finance, and was an imaginative risk-taker. I began to recognize that, like him, I actually possessed many assets — spiritual assets. My challenge was to transform these intangible resources into immediate cash. This insight galvanized me so that I could move forward and take specific actions.

The initial step toward finding your value and passion is to recognize the treasure trove of spiritual assets within you. Perhaps you take your greatest assets for granted, often believing that you don't have them. Perhaps you undervalue yourself, believing that you have little to contribute. If you are unaware of your inner gifts, they may never be expressed. You must break through your limiting beliefs and commit to the intention of being prosperous. It cannot happen without your determination.

Right now, before moving on, take a few moments to connect with your wise inner self. Envision a beautiful lotus bud, and as you repeat the affirmation "My inner wealth blossoms now" silently or aloud, imagine the bud opening up more and more, until it fully blooms as a beautiful flower. Then imagine bringing the energy of that beautiful blossom into your heart so that it's always with you.

EXERCISES FOR YOUR SOUL

The following three exercises will assist you in valuing your spiritual assets.

MANAGING YOUR SPIRITUAL PORTFOLIO
Value Your Spiritual Assets

Out of the spiritual assets listed on page 40, make a list of three talents you possess or wish you could acquire that call to you most strongly. As you did in the exercise for selling a spiritual asset on eBay, put a value on these talents. What have you done to develop them? How could you increase their value?

1.
2.
3.

PERSONAL EXPERIENCE
Choose Three Assets to Activate

Focusing on the three talents listed in step 1, as well as on your other spiritual assets, decide which ones you'd have to activate in order to achieve the most important goals in your life. How would you use them? Notice if you're having difficulty either in selecting assets to use or in determining how they might best be used.

1.

2.

3.

MEDITATION

Activate Your Spiritual Assets

Sit quietly in a comfortable position. Close your eyes and breathe easily. As you enter a calm, meditative state, mentally review two of the most important goals in your life. Do you want more love in your life? Greater prosperity? Greater happiness? Or simply a better job or place to live?

Now turn your attention inward and focus on your inner wealth of spiritual assets. Envision each one first as a shiny coin, then as a diamond, and then as a powerful white light that represents your creativity. Decide which of your spiritual assets, such as your musical ability or social intelligence, you would like to activate in order to achieve your two most important goals. How would you use them? What would you expect to happen?

Notice if it's difficult to either select which assets to use or determine how it might feel to use them. Take your time and allow yourself to be fully absorbed in the experience. See what comes to mind. Finish the meditation by focusing on your heart.

3

YOUR SPIRITUAL CAPITAL

Where Purpose Meets Intention

Intention is not something that you do. It is a force that exists in
the universe as a field of energy — a force that can carry us.

— WAYNE W. DYER, *The Power of Intention*

A re you ready? Feeling enthusiastic? Open to the possibility that
there's a fulfilling opportunity for you that could pay you well?
Having completed an inventory and discovered the true value of
your spiritual assets (everything we've looked at that falls into the
four categories of intuition and guidance, creativity, higher personality traits, and cultivated skills and knowledge), you are now
in the perfect position to set in motion a powerful force capable
of rearranging the universe. That force is love, the currency of the
soul. First you must learn how to begin investing your spiritual
assets by doing things that fulfill you, as this improves your odds
of being handsomely rewarded. After describing a formula to activate intentions, I'll discuss what could happen if you redefine
your personal goals in terms of a deeper connection to others.

Until now, you may never have thought of your spiritual assets as "investable" capital. However, if you've ever bartered your

goods or services, or if you've invested hours and effort in getting a project or business off the ground without initially drawing a salary, you're familiar with this type of personal investment. *Sweat equity* is a term used by charitable organizations like Habitat for Humanity as well as early-stage companies to describe the contribution of time and labor that people make in return for receiving material goods, such as newly constructed houses. Yet in the practical world, where money seems more real than the inner qualities that create it, this type of investment is not always respected and is often interpreted by bankers and outside investors as simply meaning: "No money was put in."

How far from the truth that explanation is. It accounts not for the immense value of the human spirit but only for cash. In fact, your inner qualities — your spiritual assets like insight, persistence, and generosity — will bring you returns that exponentially exceed material possessions and money alone.

Author J. K. Rowling is one of the clearest contemporary examples of the importance of investing your spiritual assets in an enterprise you love. What if six-year-old Joanne had been scolded every time she wrote a fantasy story about rabbits in her diary? What if she had been counseled to go into "something more practical" than the field of literature? Then Rowling might not have written *Harry Potter and the Sorcerer's Stone*, one of the most wildly successful books of all time. Rowling invested her spiritual assets — a wonderful imagination, a flash of inspiration that reportedly occurred during a train ride, and the persistence necessary to complete her manuscript despite rejections from several literary agents and publishers — and stayed focused on her intention. She wrote the first book in the Harry Potter series when she was between jobs. As a result of investing her spiritual assets in writing a children's book, Rowling went from being a writer on public assistance to becoming a billionaire and one of the wealthiest women in the world. This is the power of the phenomenon that Wall Street calls "capital formation."

Yes, like Rowling, you could become affluent by investing your spiritual assets. But it is a mistake to believe that spiritual assets should take a backseat to the tangible assets that they might create. Spirit is unlimited. So is the inherent value of your spiritual assets. You could spend your money on an unsuccessful project in which you have also invested your spiritual capital, but you may *still* come out ahead because of the greater benefits your soul will have gained — for example, greater joy, enhanced skills, and a wider network of like-minded individuals. When activated by intentionality and focus, and supercharged by passion, enthusiasm, and compassion, your invested spiritual assets become *spiritual capital*, the most potent creative force in the world.

The second step in the soul currency program is to set your intention to activate one or more of your spiritual assets by using focused intention and the multiplying power of love. The creative source of energy, love, is constantly circulating between the invisible realm of Spirit and the visible realm of matter. It is the common denominator underlying your finances and your fulfillment. As you invest your spiritual assets in your relationships and endeavors, the ways you open to the flow of love in your life will increase. Being aware of your direct connection to the source of creation adds to your sense of meaning and purpose while you set your intention to advance your career and boost your income.

As you will see a bit later in the chapter, there are reasons why investing your spiritual capital is not exactly like investing money. By enhancing, enriching, and deepening the ways you share your spiritual capital, you may change the world for the better with less effort.

INVESTING YOUR SPIRITUAL CAPITAL

In the financial world, people invest capital in order to generate a return, such as interest or dividends. Financial instruments — documents such as stocks, bonds, shares, and partnership contracts — are symbols of an agreement on the current or future value of anything from cash and physical assets (cars, buildings, machinery) to intangibles like brand names, trade secrets, copyrights, and intellectual property. These symbols are basically figments of our collective imagination and are, in reality, intangible spiritual capital that appears real to us because we have developed agreements to measure its value.

Even real estate and commodities — such as oil, wheat, precious metals (for example, gold and silver), and gemstones (for example, diamonds and emeralds) — have value only by virtue of social agreements that say they do. Our individual and collective emotional attachments to different kinds of objects and places make their value "real." In fact, the value is an illusion and is temporary.

As history has shown us, agreements as to what is valuable are changeable. In post-World-War-II Germany, paper money was inflated until it became worthless. Certain ancient Middle Eastern cultures valued silver more than gold. In 1975, the closing of a large open-pit copper mine drove housing prices in Bisbee, Arizona, down nearly 97 percent. The actual homes and properties had not changed one iota since the day before the mine closed; only their perceived value in the local real estate market had changed. I remember this well, because I was working in nearby Tombstone five years later and couldn't believe how affordable the homes were. I nearly bought one!

Spiritual capital is the only eternal form of capital, for, unlike money and other tangible assets, the source energy of love cannot be lost, destroyed, or depleted. It is only with the investment of love, the currency of the soul, that a return on human spirit may be generated. Of course, the word *return* is really a misnomer when describing spiritual capital, because love infuses everything. As you will see, more and greater aspects of love are revealed whenever and wherever love is invested. In addition, where love is invested, you also can create the symbols of wealth, such as money, real estate, and securities.

Using your inner qualities is a bit like conducting an orchestra. Like an orchestra, you could choose to play something short and simple or to undertake a symphony of magnificent proportions. As you develop greater awareness and self-mastery, it will take less effort to do either, and the rewards will be higher. How you invest your spiritual assets is guided by intuition and by the self-organizing power of spiritual intelligence, two important spiritual assets.

Investment of spiritual assets is set into motion by the power of intentionality, which is then directed by positive focus. The energy of love is a multiplication factor that augments the investment, transforming it into greater spiritual capital that brings dividends. If you are one of those people who find formulas helpful, you could state this principle in the form of an equation: $SC = (F + I + SA)^L$. In other words, spiritual capital equals focus plus intention plus spiritual assets, multiplied exponentially by love.

THE FIELD OF INTENTIONALITY

Imagine that you could plug yourself into a socket that would tap into the electric current of the universe. Because source energy is indivisible and boundless, this would give you access to such an unlimited supply of energy that only you could limit or stop its flow. Well, in fact, you are plugged in, and you are responsible for the level of flow you experience.

Our individual intentions connect us to a deeper field of intentionality that is one aspect of universal source energy. As such, it is limitless and connects us to everything that exists. Our inner field of intentionality has an intelligence that naturally opens us to the highest and best outcome in every given situation. It marshals the best of our inner qualities to bring a potential outcome into reality. And it taps into the universal field to draw opportunities toward us.

What's the difference between an intention and intentionality? A butterfly could have the intention to alight on a flower and feed on its nectar. Intentionality is built into the monarch butterfly species, whose members all travel up to three thousand miles in order to spend the winter in a mild climate. The apple tree that springs from the tiny seed within a rotting apple demonstrates intentionality, whereas its intention may be to turn a single leaf so that it reaches for the sunlight. Intentionality is built into the wave that breaks on the shore. An intention may be to use that wave to bodysurf.

Intentionality is the blueprint that connects us to the cocreative energy of the universe. At the moment you experience a creative thought, your conscious mind is sending an intention rippling through the field of intentionality. This thought contributes to the direction that divine energy will flow and express itself. After all, everything around you is energy and a part of the same blueprint that you are part of. If you choose to drive home along a different route than you normally do, for example, you are creating an entirely new set of possibilities for yourself and for the universal energy. You might see a car that has a flat tire by the edge of the road. A thoughtless driver might cut you off. You could get lost and have a number of experiences as a result. The cocreative universe automatically fills in the possibilities that flow back to you.

The field of quantum physics suggests that nothing happens by chance or by accident, and that everything in existence is interconnected.[1] The energy of the "real" world (source energy) shape-shifts into the landscape of our reality. One condition or choice affects another, which affects another, and then what you experience as tangible "reality" emerges. Our power to affect reality in specific ways is magnified by the clarity of our thoughts and the intensity of our feelings. That's how we activate the shared field of divine intelligence.

Quantum physics has shown that the field of intentionality is part of a unified field of consciousness. Dr. Masaru Emoto has done pioneering research on the effects of intention and energy on frozen water crystals. In his book *The Hidden Messages in Water*, he describes how words and phrases such as "love" and "thank you" create clear and symmetrical water crystals and words and phrases such as "I want to kill you" or "Hitler" create broken, asymmetrical, and murky frozen water crystals. On his website you can see many more photographic examples.[2] Emoto also has documented the power of intentionality by having groups use prayer to clear polluted lakes and streams, and by having individuals use prayer to help plants grow.

Dr. Robert Jahn, dean emeritus and former professor of aerospace engineering at Princeton University's School of Engineering and Applied Science, established that patterns of random numbers could be affected by the intentions or beliefs of experimenters. Furthermore, he has shown that random number generators located in different parts of the globe are also tapped into the unified field of intentionality. Much like the equipment that measures earthquakes, on several occasions they have shown unusually high spikes. These occasions coincided with world events such as the death of Princess Diana, the 9/11 bombings in 2001, and the Indonesian tsunami in 2004.

Journalist Lynne McTaggart, author of *The Intention Experiment*, has documented that the energy of collective intentionality can lower crime statistics and reduce accidents at dangerous intersections. On the individual level, young athletes were able to build up their biceps by visualizing this intention — without exercise. Apparently the human body can act as a sort of biological antenna, as it is capable of transmitting and receiving focused healing intentions.

Part of the process of developing your awareness of soul currency is to redefine your intentions in terms of connection and unity rather than separation. Your good is the good of the world, because your personal biofield — the magnetic and spiritual energy that sustains your life and emanates from you — is connected to all life-forms around you. Reflect for a moment upon everyone you come into contact with in the course of an average day. Were you aware of sending them loving (or hostile) thoughts? Did you feel or express gratitude for the people?

Notice whether you were a healing presence or simply chose not to have an intention. The next time you interact with others, notice how your body feels. Does any part of your body feel uncomfortable? Or is it relaxed and open?

If you're not clear about an intention, then things won't show up. There will be delays. Growing your spiritual capital isn't about working harder, but about being more closely aligned with Spirit. When you sit and do a daily reflection or meditation, allow an intention to come into your awareness. As it comes, scan your body. How does it feel? If there's tightness, your self-preserving ego is probably involved. If you're relaxed, your intuition is more likely to be operating.

You can test an intention by the opportunities that show up when you start focusing on it. It's like buying a car, such as a Volkswagen Jetta. You never see one until you get interested in them, then you see them everywhere. If you are hung up on form and on how your spiritual capital should look, you might miss the flow coming back to you. Being open to receive is more important than putting stuff out. Because the universe reflects you, when you shine a light inside yourself and give to yourself, immediately the universe pours more energy into you.

ACTIVATING YOUR SPIRITUAL ASSETS BY FOCUSING

The field of intentionality is what makes goal-setting processes work in life and in business, and it's responsible for any particular occasion on which you may recall asserting, "When I *really* make up my mind that I want something, I get it!" But even the greatest intentions go nowhere unless they are activated by focus, because the field is responsive. It requires clear instructions to take a particular form.

The energy of the universe is pure potential, except when there is a thought. Focusing on a thought starts a reorganizing process in the field of intentionality that we share in common. Most startling is that, despite the trillions of thoughts of the billions of people on Earth, our focused thoughts create order out of the seeming chaos. How can the universe support everyone's intentions at the same time? Because everyone and everything is part of a unified energy field, which is interdimensional, aware, and responsive to thought.

Focus is a spiritual asset. We often call it by other names: determination, attention, commitment, concentration, single-mindedness, and obsession are among them. These names have all been used to describe various degrees of the focus that we bring to bear on the needs of the moment, but essentially they all refer to the same spiritual asset.

Focus also is the process of noticing in present time. Although it relates to intentionality, it is the process by which you clear your mind and connect with the greater intelligence of the source of creation. When your mind is truly present, your intuition will speak to you in clearer, louder tones, and you'll notice that events in your life flow more synchronistically.

Management guru Peter Senge, in the book *Presence*, observes, "We first thought of presence as being fully conscious and aware in the present moment. Then we began to appreciate presence as deep listening, of being open beyond one's preconceptions and historical ways of making sense. We came to see the importance of letting go of old identities and the need to control."[3]

The great American business philosopher Jim Rohn in *The Treasury of Quotes*, writes, "Pay attention. Don't just stagger through the day."[4] Try making the choice to focus upon one intention for a couple of days and see what happens in your life. Many of the students in my abundance course get excited when they discover that virtually everything they do, everyone that they meet, and everything they learn seems to apply to their intentions when they test their focus this way.

Focus is like having a conversation with Spirit, as it opens up a two-way channel of creative energy and intuitive listening. The trick — if you can call it that — is taking the messages you receive seriously. Look around you. There are many examples of how focus guides the lives of people you know. My eldest son, Chris Chu, is proof that focus pays dividends over a period of time (sometimes it takes weeks, sometimes years). At age ten, he was fascinated by the action and creativity of computer video games. Like millions of other children, he spent hours playing Myst and Halo, fantasy games that offer players multiple options and involve the idea of going on journeys. The images and the stories equally fascinated him. Soon he announced his intention to become a video game programmer. Through the years, he stayed focused on this singular objective by teaching himself advanced math and computer programming. By the time Chris got to high school, he probably could have taught courses on these subjects better than his schoolteachers.

Out of a passion for knowledge, Chris read books on quantum physics when he was fourteen. He still thoroughly enjoyed interactive gaming, and his deepening understanding of experimental physics and math enabled him to see possibilities for the design of new and improved video games. When he went to California State Polytechnic University in Pomona, California, the academic advisors placed him in senior-level courses during his freshman year. Eventually, he ran out of courses to take in his chosen subject area and dropped out of college with two semesters left to complete. He immediately joined a small video game software firm, which allowed him hands-on experience in designing major projects, like Shrek, Call of Duty, and others.

By the time Chris was twenty-four, fourteen years after he set his original intention to be a game designer, he had a wealth of programming experience and knew as much as programmers ten years his senior. In 2006, as one of the senior programmers at Activision, he was a key member of the small team that won the Academy Award for Best Sound in a Video Game for the game Call of Duty 3, the only award his company received that year. Applying focus to the individual microsteps and basic information required in order to work in the field he loved gradually brought him success and joy.

Focus with presence allows us to connect with the energy of the universe. Everyone has the ability to focus, even people diagnosed with attention deficit disorder (ADD), who are known to have trouble organizing sensory input. A person with ADD, such as myself, can often sustain a single-minded focus for many hours at a time, shutting out all other distractions. Without exception we all get better at focusing on present-time tasks as we practice this, and as we master the different techniques that support intense focus.

For a moment, allow yourself to reflect upon occasions when you got caught up in an activity and perhaps lost the sense of time passing. What were you doing that captivated you? Are you capable of focusing on specific tasks for reasonable periods of time? Focusing on a specific intention even for short periods of time every day — perhaps as few as ten minutes — anchors that intention in your subconscious mind. The phrase *subconscious mind* refers to the unconscious beliefs and spirit within that act upon our thoughts to produce our emotions and actions. Your focus is the fuel that propels your dreams forward.

So how could you launch an actual intention? One way is to write it down on a small piece of paper that you can tuck into your wallet and carry around with you. The written word is very powerful, especially if you go back and read it at various intervals. Posting a list of affirmations pertaining to your intention in a place where you'll see them frequently, such as on the bathroom mirror or on the refrigerator door, also keeps your mind focused on the end result. Some examples are: "My inner wealth blossoms now," "I am grateful for receiving more and more good each day," and "I attract only love and prosperity."

This works for groups, too. The United Way of Cincinnati activated the field of intentionality by declaring a group intention. It then posted a "donation thermometer" online and hung its physical counterpart in a highly visible location to constantly remind participants and potential donors of the goal. The charity raised more than $62,830,000 in 2007.

Saying your affirmations aloud while looking in the mirror is a technique that compels more of your brain to participate in grounding an intention in reality. We all have stronger and weaker senses, so taking advantage of the power of all our physical senses to make us believe in the possibility of a goal being realized is important. We benefit from thinking it, hearing it, and seeing it — even feeling it — as real. Many highly visual people find the creation of treasure maps or dream posters — collages of inspiring words and pictures clipped from magazines — useful in focusing. Every time you cast your eyes on your artwork, it will remind you of your intention.

Being conscious about your intention in quiet moments during the day, and entering your thoughts and feelings about your intention in a journal, are two more ways to invest your love in, and focus on, the preferred outcome.

THE EXPONENTIAL POWER OF LOVE

Love, the source energy of Spirit, is the final element in our formula for the creation of spiritual capital: $SC = (F + I + SA)^L$. Love takes the energy of our inner gifts and resources and multiplies it exponentially. It is a remarkable experience when the floodgates of love are opened. Once love is added to the mixture, it's as if we've made an investment in a five-dollar stock and now see it rise in a flash to over one hundred dollars a share. Love helps us create flows of money, of volunteers, and of professional connections that can enable us, as individuals, to create programs and products that reach and serve tens of millions of people worldwide.

Interestingly, love cannot be faked. Remember that love is source energy. You may experience it as a feeling, but its overall power is creative. Because it's so much a part of you, whenever you feel love you feel as if you are dancing with the Divine. Love, as the creative source, both moves through you and is you. You are in harmony with the flow of the universe. When you are the right person at the right time and the right place, then you can see and feel and know the intelligence of the source of creation, which is expressed through us so wisely.

Often the multiplying power of love is released through catalyzing events in our lives, such as a tragedy that invites change, commands a response, and inspires courage. Dark nights of the soul open the flow of love in our lives. An example of this extraordinary phenomenon is Kenny Kramm. At age twenty-nine, Kenny seemed to have it all. He had married his college sweetheart, and they shared a comfortable home with their three-year-old daughter near Bethesda, Maryland. Kramm was ensconced as a pharmacy technician in the family business, an old-fashioned pharmacy run by his father that he expected to eventually take over. Then came the biggest challenge of his life: his second daughter, Hadley, only ten days old, began having seizures, possibly resulting from a massive brain hemorrhage. The beautiful little girl was diagnosed with multiple disorders, in-cluding a blood-clotting disorder, continuing seizures, and cere-bral palsy.

Heartbroken, Kenny and his wife did their best to get Hadley to gulp down the awful-tasting medicines required to manage her seizures and cerebral palsy. She would immediately spit them out or, if she swallowed them, throw up. Desperate to ensure that his daughter would take the life-saving medicine, Kramm began experimenting with harmless additives and flavors. After nearly a dozen tries with candy flavorings, he found one that worked: banana.

Kramm realized that many other parents faced similar strug-gles with their children. So he began experimenting with other flavors to improve the taste of often-prescribed medicines in liquid, pill, or powder form. Seeking to help others, Kramm activated the multiplying power of love.

His pharmacy was located in a building that housed several pediatricians and an annex of the Children's Hospital National Medical Center. Pretty soon, as Hadley's story spread, doctors began sending patients, including adults, to him to have their prescriptions filled and flavored. For Kramm, who had taken business courses in college, this was an opportunity not only to increase the pharmacy's sales volume but also to assuage the heartache he felt as he treated his own child day after day. The greater idea of helping children everywhere spurred him on.

The love Kenny Kramm and his wife have for Hadley engendered FLAVORx Inc., now the leader in flavorings for medicines. The additional revenue from FLAVORx has paid for the extremely high costs of Hadley's continuing treatment. The company now offers more than forty flavoring choices, including bubble gum and licorice, as well as standard fruit and candy flavorings, and has added flavorings for cats and dogs who won't take vile-tasting medicine any more readily than most children. The company's products now reach thousands of families thanks to distribution agreements with Kroger, Winn-Dixie, and other major drugstore and pharmacy chains.

Mother Teresa once said, "It is not the magnitude of our actions but the amount of love that is put into them that matters."[5] Love, as the multiplication factor of spiritual capital, is not just about corporate success or prosperity but is also about wholeness and connection. You release it through passion, enthusiasm, intention to serve, and other catalysts that allow you to be filled with love and joy.

THREE LEVELS OF SPIRITUAL INVESTMENT

How you choose to invest your spiritual assets — and why — determines the richness of your resulting experience and what is created by your investment. For example, do you choose to make safe, short-term investments that produce direct and even measurable returns for you? Do you invest in bigger ideas that are not necessarily correlated with direct returns? Or do you give away or share your spiritual capital out of love without ever expecting a return?

There are three levels of consciousness that lead to three types of intentionality. Most of us experience these levels in different moments. The energy it takes to sustain the higher levels of consciousness is geometrically more potent and creative than at the lower levels.

Self-Cherishing Consciousness

The Dalai Lama coined the phrase *self-cherishing* to describe someone whose level of intention is primarily self-motivated. You intend to go to the grocery store or get to work early. You intend to find a parking space in a busy shopping mall. Such intentions are neither malicious nor necessarily harmful; they are just solitary. And they rarely lead to massive expansions of opportunity and income.

When your investments of spiritual assets, such as your imagination and your artistry, are made to pursue self-cherishment intentions, you'll generate mixed returns. Your thoughts are likely to vacillate between succeeding and failing because you're focused on the outcome. You might fear putting too much time into a project without seeing immediate benefits, largely because you attach your self-worth to the outcome of your efforts. Like a Wall Street venture capitalist, you'll weigh risk versus reward before taking on a new project. If things don't work out, you might have investor's remorse.

People who choose to invest purely for self-benefit appear to be at the mercy of outside influences beyond their control. Spiritual capital generated at this level of intentionality emerges from effort, determination, and will, rather than from creativity, flow, and expansiveness. Fulfillment comes from material rewards, not the multitude of inner rewards that are more lasting measurements of success. Because the focus is on the future outcome, worrying about the next step blocks both the genuine enjoyment of the moment and one's trust in inner guidance.

Connection Consciousness

The most powerful form of thought is the intention that connects us to something much bigger than ourselves — a family, a community, a nation, a planet, the universe, God, and all creation. An intention at this level is an invitation to unleash the glimmers of greatness within you. Subconsciously or consciously, it can become the core mission of your life. You intend to cocreate a world that supports you and creates both personal expansion and flow — the least of which is money. While you may also choose to focus on "practical" daily activities and short-term goals, you intend to invest your spiritual assets in an idea, activity, or grand purpose. You are connected to the larger you.

When investments of spiritual assets are made from the perspective of soul-connection, the intentionality is rooted in giving and sharing, and the return on your investments is likely to be oriented to a long-term vision rather than short-term results. When you share your gifts from the deepest part of your being — the larger you — you tap into the invisible flow that connects all of life. On the inside, you feel passionate and enthusiastic, because you've opened a channel for your soul to express love and creativity in a signature style.

Spiritual capital generated by soul-connected consciousness

is related to what you contribute to life rather than to doing a particular job. The way that the late Jim Henson, creator of *The Muppet Show*, expressed his love by investing humor and creativity in projects designed to educate children is an example of soul-connected investment.

Seva Consciousness

Seva is the spiritual practice of selfless service. From this level of consciousness, which arises out of the yogic traditions, emerges the intentionality of giving without an expectation of return. Seva, from the Sanskrit word that has come to mean "selfless service," is the essence of philanthropy: the sharing of the innermost gifts you have, for the good of others. You intend to imbue your actions with love. You intend to be there as the need arises. You serve as a divine practice. You have realized there is no separation between Spirit and self, no separation between self and all other life.

The true richness generated by how you manage your spiritual capital at this level of consciousness and intentionality is a reflection of your acceptance of Spirit's call to accept the greater you. It is an invitation to throw aside the "me" mentality and understand that everything is an aspect of the One. At this level there is no self, only one magnificent whole entity.

In his book, *Leaving Microsoft to Change the World*, entrepreneur John Wood talks about the hiking vacation he planned to take in order to chill out from his high-stress job as a Microsoft marketing executive. Underneath that purpose, he had a greater intention: to find meaning in his life. He found an outlet for his enthusiasm and talents when he decided to take some additional time off from work to clear his mind. He signed up to go to Nepal and hike in the Himalayas. By chance he met a Nepalese guide whose job it was to oversee remote elementary schools. Asking if he could come along to visit one such school, Wood noticed that the school's library possessed only a few books left behind by hikers. Most of them were not suitable for young kids, even though the children were eager to learn. The library was bare. Realizing that he could make a difference, he left with the commitment to bring back a yakload of books from America.

Seva intentionality has the power to muster virtually unlimited support. When Wood sent out an email to his network of friends and colleagues requesting help, he got inundated with books and financial contributions. He began to realize that his intention to find greater purpose and meaning in his life would be realized in the form of a nonprofit organization. He soon resigned his position at Microsoft and established Room to Read, an organization with a mission to foster literacy in countries where few children have the opportunity to get a good education. Room to Read has since established dozens of schools in Nepal, Vietnam, and other nations. Today, Wood continues to be an advocate for this nonprofit's vision for enriching children.

Like Wood, Dr. Dan Carlson, an agricultural scientist from Minnesota, stumbled across his life's purpose by responding to a need with his unique blend of spiritual assets. He is further proof that life is self-organizing, that it directs the soul's currency to establish confluences of love, intention, guidance, and destiny. Stationed in the demilitarized zone of Korea in 1960, Carlson, a U.S. Army private attached to a motor pool, watched in horror as a poor Korean woman with two small children deliberately put one of her four-year-old son's legs beneath the tires of an American supply truck as it backed up. Unable to prevent the child's leg from being crushed permanently, Carlson turned his anger on the woman, only to learn that she had no way to feed her children. The relatively small compensation she would receive for her son's crushed leg would allow her to collect enough money to feed her starving family.

The situation moved the burly young GI to tears. The sight of the desperate mother crippling her son so her family would receive food subsidies so shocked Carlson that he made a vow that he would devote his life to finding an answer to hunger so that children would be fed, and mothers would never again make this terrible kind of choice. This specific intention became the core mission of his life. When he returned to the United States, he pursued a doctorate in agriculture and began a research project called Sonic Bloom, which led to new insights into how to stimulate plant growth using sound and innovative nutrients. Years later, Carlson has created "supercrops" that produce greater yields and fruit trees that have extra fruit-bearing seasons.

Carlson recently donated more than $4 million worth of seeds treated by Sonic Bloom to the government of Indonesia, which is expecting them to produce more than 100 million kilos of food for its people, many of whom are impoverished and suffering from malnourishment.[6] Despite toiling in relative obscurity, Carlson has received several lifetime achievement awards and was nominated for the Nobel Peace Prize in 2001 and 2004, representing the high value of his spiritual capital.

Would you like to cultivate selflessness, especially if you feel that you're a little bit more self-cherishing than you'd like to admit in public? Then pay attention to the intentions you set for your interactions with others. Notice if you are solitary or connected. Your desire for connection will prompt growth. Every day you may catch glimpses of selfless service or philanthropy in yourself when holding the door open for someone else, giving an encouraging word, or simply smiling. In doing these things, you express and model love and allow it to circulate throughout the planet. This is one of the easiest ways to begin developing more valuable spiritual capital.

FIVE KEYS TO EXPANDING
YOUR SPIRITUAL CAPITAL

How could you more effectively manage your spiritual capital? Do you scatter it like a spendthrift, allowing your intention and focus to be divided among a great many things? Are you mistaking activity for effectiveness? Are you spending more time "doing" (and being attached to the results of your activities) than you spend laying a foundation composed of your inner being, upon which you can build? Spiritual intelligence is the ultimate awareness that guides you in how you utilize and blend your spiritual assets. It is the wisdom that enables you to discern whether one course of action or life path is more meaningful than another. Let this intelligence manage your soul's investment plan.

Here are five suggestions for unleashing the power of your spiritual capital.

- Keep your word. "In the beginning was the word," says the book of Genesis in the Bible, describing God's first act of creation. What you say is a form of spiritual capital investment, an act of creation. The power of your soul is accessed through your thoughts, declarations, and agreements — your word. Since the world reflects back to you what is within you, you need to be careful to keep your word, especially to yourself. Otherwise you may find your goals delayed or may attract partners or friends who have difficulty keeping their agreements.

  Something as seemingly simple as being on time may be not only an issue of courtesy but may also reveal the thought and importance you give to the agreements you make. As one of my earliest spiritual teachers once told me, "If you want the world to be on time for you, then be on time for the world." If you consistently tend to overcommit, notice how this contributes to creating situations in which it becomes difficult or impossible to fulfill your agreements. Look also at some of the feelings behind your overcommitment, such as self-sabotage, the desire for approval, or something else. If you're unable to keep an agreement, renegotiate it before your deadline, and develop the habit of underpromising and overdelivering.

- **Commit.** American inventor Thomas Edison has often been quoted as saying, "Most people miss opportunity because it is dressed in overalls and looks like work."[7] His commitment to his work was legendary. Napoleon Hill, in *Think and Grow Rich*, comments on Edison's repeated, unsuccessful efforts to make an incandescent lightbulb: "Thomas Edison 'failed' 10,000 times before he perfected the incandescent electric light bulb — that is, he met with *temporary defeat* 10,000 times before his efforts were crowned with success."[8] Edison ate, drank, and slept his project, so it was no accident that a dream showed him that, when he removed air from the bulb, the filament would give off light without burning up. Commitment is discipline, the backbone of intention. When you express your commitment by showing up and doing what needs to be done time after time after time, you release the energy of your spiritual capital into the world.

Interestingly, although commitment may show up as "doing," its source is a state of being. My friend Carol Reed Bamesberger is a certified Catholic chaplain who has spent more than twenty-seven years setting up care organizations for HIV-positive and AIDS-infected children and their families and for clergy with AIDS. Her commitment began when she had a stroke while shopping in a grocery store.

She remembers lying on the floor unable to see very well and whispering a request for help while the other shoppers avoided her, believing she was drunk or deranged. Having experienced being helpless, she later was able to imagine the feelings of loneliness and helplessness of ostracized AIDS patients. Over the next eight months, along with making a miraculous recovery, she committed herself to providing a safe, caring environment for HIV and AIDS patients. This resulted in the formation of the Angel Connection, a now twenty-year-old organization that provides social and spiritual services for children and families in need.[9]

- Look for the greater lesson, not the form. Environmental activist and author John Robbins turned his back on the family business, Baskin-Robbins, one of the world's major ice cream producers. His family's resources had afforded him a Harvard education, ostensibly to groom him to be president of the company. But he believed that ice cream contributed to our disharmony with our environment. He reasoned that herds of cattle consume a hugely disproportionate amount of water, and that dairy products and beef contribute to the epidemic of heart attacks, strokes, and cardiovascular disease. John shunned corporate America and instead wrote the Pulitzer Prize–winning book *Diet for a New America*.

    Contrast Robbins's decision with that of two other entrepreneurs who share many of his values, Ben Cohen and Jerry Greenfield, who grew up together in Merrick, New York, and went on to cofound the highly profitable ice cream company Ben & Jerry's. They support the idea of a green economy, one that includes the recycling of resources and elimination of toxic landfills. Yet from childhood they were passionate about ice cream and saw an opportunity to have fun and make money concocting yummy mixtures with such names as Chubby Hubby, Cookie Dough, and Chunky Monkey. Until their retirement, Ben and Jerry practiced what they believe by maintaining an environmentally and socially conscious business. The company was sold to Unilever, a large international consumer products company, in April 2000. Although its management style is more corporate, the company still tries to maintain the legacy of its founders.

As you begin building your spiritual capital, focus on contributing your spiritual assets rather than on being attached to the form in which your returns come back to you. Remember that the field of intentionality is cocreating with you — you create conditions, not outcomes.

- Invest love. When we invest spiritual assets, they become spiritual capital — activated and magnified. In a world that is primarily invisible, love is the prima facie currency. Investing love in the universal flow allows us to become the vibration of that currency. Love itself is magnified as it moves through us. Furthermore, your mind becomes an expression of love, rather than an expression of a sea of other emotions from among which you select love.

Inventor John Kanzius, after being diagnosed with a form of terminal leukemia, underwent regular chemotherapy sessions. In an interview with *60 Minutes*, he related that he had visited a children's ward where many children had terminal cancer. He had seen the emptiness in their eyes and been moved by how the disease and the toxic chemotherapy treatments had robbed them of their vitality. John used his ingenuity and his background — he had invented radio-frequency communication systems — to develop a method to destroy cancer cells without harming the cells around them. A leading cancer researcher has already tested the method, which appears to be exceptionally promising. Kanzius is still searching for a cure for his own terminal blood disorder, but by investing his spiritual capital he may have extended the lives of potentially millions of people with tumor-related cancers.[10]

The greatest vehicles for the investment of love are ways of being, not doing. Investing love means maintaining a conscious state of being — a habit that becomes second nature. If you come across someone having difficulty in his or her life, you can either wonder, "When is he or she ever going to get his or her act together?" or send loving thoughts, seeing a vision of that person's success and simply knowing that all is well for him or her.

Another way to invest love is simply to be "out of your mind" with love. Love is a way of being. When you are in your mind, you're inhabiting your self-cherishing ego. But scientists have shown that, when you are in love, the spaces between your cells literally expand. When you allow loving energy to become you, your friends will notice that your face seems to radiate happiness or that you are lighter. Love is not something you "try" to do; rather it's something that's already a part of you. When I say it's a good investment, I mean that it's really the only authentic investment you can make.

- Embrace change. You are in a constant state of creative transformation. This means that you can always feel the energy of change underlying your life, although it may not be as noticeable in one moment as it is in the next. As the old gives way to the new, many of us find change uncomfortable. For some people, it's the speed of change that's uncomfortable — when, for example, you're uprooted from your home because of a disaster, or need to change jobs in a hurry, or have a sudden major change in a relationship. For others, it's handling unfamiliarity and wondering, "Where do we go from here?"

To embrace change, you must accept that a power for good inside you knows exactly what to do. It requires you to embrace yourself as a reflection of Spirit in circulation. Change doesn't just come to you as an outside event: it's first created within you and then mirrored. To be afraid of what you see in the mirror is to be afraid of Spirit, the essence of who you are. By challenging the frightened and resisting parts of your personality, you can learn to see change as moving you in the direction of your highest and best spiritual growth.

YOUR NEW INVESTMENT STRATEGY

Your spiritual capital is creative, alive, and more powerful than money, because it's infused with the source energy of love. Financial capital, on the other hand, is static, because the symbols of value in the world of finance gain their worth by agreement, rather than from the energy of value *itself*. Because spiritual capital is alive and composed of source energy, you invest spiritual capital in a process quite different from the way you'd invest financial capital.

The Internet is a perfect example of how the search engines reward the investment of spiritual capital by giving valuable information or products first, rather than just offering sales pitches. The more content-driven the site is, the higher the rankings. The most successful Internet marketers, such as Matt Bacak and Armand Morin, give away large amounts of meaningful content for free.

Blue Mountain Arts, a company started by artist Susan Polis Shultz and her husband is another example of the rewards of investing spiritual capital. Greeting cards containing her moving poems are offered for free on the company's website. Her broad selection and special cards catapulted the site to one of the top ten most-visited sites, surpassing a competitive subscription site offered by American Greetings. Neither of the founders could have predicted that the company would be bought for more than $780 million several years later by Excite@Home.[11]

In the financial world, financial objectives determine the investment strategy. For example, an older person who needs to live off the returns of an investment portfolio generally will invest in bonds, dividend-paying high-quality securities, and high-quality conservative stocks that have stability and modest growth. These might be blue-chip stocks, utilities, and triple-A-rated companies. A younger person typically will choose to invest in high-growth stocks, and mutual funds or other securities. These are riskier investments than the older person would make. The primary concern of financial investment strategy is the element of risk.

Risk measurement, of course, encompasses the energy of fear and loss. Stock market value is heavily influenced by the currents of fear and greed, often leading to wide swings in the broad financial averages, as well as in the value of stocks themselves. Therefore a conservative investment strategy is to minimize or diversify the risk, which usually means the investor's expectation of reward is less than it would be for a high-growth investment strategy. A high-growth strategy may involve leverage, which means borrowing capital with the expectation that the return to the lender will be a lot more than the interest on the money alone.

Since your spiritual capital is infused with the energy of love, the greatest returns come from giving this energy away with no expectation of return. The cardinal rule of investing spiritual capital is to give and give some more, knowing that you can't out-give Spirit. Love always provides a return that is exponentially greater than an unconditional gift.

If you invest your spiritual capital conditionally, your returns will be smaller and they'll have conditions attached to them. This happens in business all the time, when one colleague holds his or her contacts so close to the vest that others stop sharing their contacts with him or her. The colleague becomes isolated, because people recognize him or her as a taker and not a giver. If you conserve your spiritual capital, your returns will be conserved as well. The impulse to conserve spiritual capital is usually tinged with fear, risk aversion, and limitation, and this may result in a limited return and even the illusion of loss. Therefore the most "conservative" investment strategy to adopt for your spiritual capital is the opposite of the strategy you'd adopt for investing financial capital. Investing your spiritual capital without being attached to the amount of the return opens the flow of return.

TRUST THE SOURCE

The wellspring of our spiritual capital gushes whenever we choose to invest our inner resources with focused intentionality. Because our inner gifts actually are aspects of the Divine Spirit, we always — under any conditions and for whatever reason we choose — have access to source energy in the form of raw potential. By using the catalysts of passion and inspiration, we can intensify, enrich, and deepen the power of our spiritual capital. Then we can reshape it into forms that we experience as having greater value and deeper connection, purpose, and fulfillment. The only thing we must remember is that source energy flows in nonlinear ways.

It may be difficult to grasp that you are responsible for the creation of your abundance and fulfillment. If you work for a company, you might think your job creates money. But in fact, your spiritual capital sets in motion a shift in the conditions and circumstances that made it possible for you to get the job in the first place. If your focus is on money, the universe responds in the swiftest way it can by seeing that you receive a timely tax refund check or monies that are owed to you. The universe's response might also show up in nonmonetary ways that can be converted into money, such as when you find something of value that you thought was lost, are given a present, or create a situation that gives you an opportunity to make money by representing a product or person.

If you're an entrepreneur, you may be able to see clearly the direct influence on your flow when one of your spiritual assets helps you land a new customer, or a million-dollar idea pops into your mind, or you just happen to be in the right place at the right time. As mentioned earlier, nothing happens by accident. Everything is created at one time or another through the investment of your inner spiritual resources and the spiritual capital you've accumulated.

Source energy is always available for you to draw on. It's never too late to discover it, whether you create a situation in which there is a dire need for you to shine, or whether you're empowered by your imagination, a vision, or new ideas that just seem to pop into your mind. The more you learn to value your spiritual assets, the more the world will reflect that great value back to you. You can trust that your focused intentions will activate what mythologist Joseph Campbell has called the "invisible hands" of the universe and economist Adam Smith has described as the "invisible hand" of the marketplace.[12]

EXERCISES FOR YOUR SOUL

The following three exercises will assist you in understanding the power of your spiritual capital.

MANAGING YOUR SPIRITUAL PORTFOLIO

Set Your Top Six Investment Goals

On a clean sheet of paper, write down six goals, one for each of the following six areas of your life: health, relationships, work, money, spirituality, and home. Example: "I choose vibrant health." Leave a few blank lines between goals, so you'll have room to make notes.

On a new line below each goal, explain how you plan to invest your spiritual capital (beingness) to realize that intention. Example: "My spiritual capital investment is to fill my inner self with love and to know myself as magnificent, joyful, and deserving."

Finally, on another fresh line below each goal, explain one or more actions you'll take to bring it about (doings). Your actions might be to buy a health club membership or eat organic foods.

PERSONAL EXPERIENCE

Evaluate Your Past Accomplishments and Blessings in Disguise

In the past you've had successes. You've also had moments in which you appeared to fail but really experienced a blessing. An example of a blessing in disguise is losing a job you like — a week before a scandal erupts. You can learn about yourself by examining how these past events relate to your investment of spiritual capital.

Select a moment and, using the formula for spiritual capital — $SC = (F + I + SA)^L$ — write down how you used the key elements of focus, intentionality, and love to accomplish your goals.

How I used the power of my focus:
How I used the power of my intentionality:
How I used the power of love:

MEDITATION

Identify Your Life's Underlying Mission Statement

Sit quietly on your own for ten to fifteen minutes. Reflect on the conscious and unconscious intentions that currently function as your life's mission statement. Examples: "Be safe." "Go it alone." There's no right or wrong answer. However, when you identify your driving intentions, much of what has happened in your life will start to become clearer. Envision moments in which you feel empowered, appreciated, and loved. Then envision moments when you empower, appreciate, and show love to others. Notice how you feel in these moments — especially the feelings and words that come to mind. Condense these feelings into a glowing pink orb of light that envelops you for a minute or two. Then give thanks and take this light into your heart.

ELIMINATING COUNTERFEIT CURRENCY

Downsizing the Power of Fear and False Beliefs

The opposite of love is fear, but what is all-encompassing can have no opposite.

— *A COURSE IN MIRACLES*

If you suspected you had counterfeit currency in your wallet, would you take it out of circulation, or would you pass it on? Would you see yourself as a victim for having unwittingly received it? Would you knowingly spend a fake hundred-dollar bill if you thought no one would notice? Would you see yourself as doing a public service by destroying it or turning it in to authorities? Upon reflection about why you answer as you do, your answers will reveal to you some of your underlying beliefs about scarcity and abundance, how much you feel you deserve, and your ability to receive and circulate soul currency in an unimpeded flow.

As soul currency is rooted in love, counterfeit currency is rooted in fear. Beliefs, mind-sets, and behavior based on fear are counterfeit currency. Even if you pass them on to others or invest them in your activities, they will not build spiritual capital for you. They carry the energy of pain and constriction rather than of celebration and growth. Fear (an acronym for "false expectations appearing real") creates the illusion in your mind that you are alone and separated from Spirit. Fear gives you the message that, *if* love is available to you, *then* you have to earn it. Fear pulls you into a contraction, saps your energy, and makes you feel unsafe, whereas love, the genuine currency of the soul, is expansive and life-giving, and it makes you feel joyful.

By now you're well aware that the fundamental purpose of the soul currency program is to improve the circulation of love in your life. Money, career success, healthy relationships, and personal fulfillment all come from this flowing, infinite source of goodness that can't be stopped. However, you face a choice. Either you can be like an open riverbed, intentionally guiding the energy of love so that it pours through you smoothly en route to its next destination, or you can be like a boulder-strewn riverbed, filled with a jumble of contradictory thoughts and impulses that impede the flow of love and divert it away from you and into more navigable passageways. Spirit is intelligent and always finds ways to deliver love as swiftly and effortlessly as possible.

To support your highest intentions for your life and help you open your heart to receive an abundant flow of love, the third step in the soul currency program is to reduce the power of fear in your mind. Fear is the biggest obstacle to your prosperity and fulfillment. You must also begin to pay down the spiritual debt you incurred in the past by circulating counterfeit currency in different areas of your life. By consciously choosing to embrace your connectedness to everything and everyone that exists, you can begin to intentionally express Spirit — and its action in you and your life will expand. Your self-esteem and energy will skyrocket.

True enlightenment — allegiance with the deepest reality of Spirit — comes more from a process of subtraction than it does from addition. It's about letting go of ideas of self-criticism, fear, and separation from Spirit, not about having more or doing more. It's about *being* more of who you are and allowing your natural, soulful radiance to shine forth, about uncovering what is shuttered, shaded, and painted over to disguise its appearance. Your spiritual capital effortlessly increases when your divine aspects are expressed, because they are naturally valuable.

WHY THE CURRENCY OF FEAR IS COUNTERFEIT

Let me be clear that, when I describe fear, I'm not referring to the healthy type of self-preserving fear that would arise if someone sneaked up behind you in a dark alley to crack you over the head with a tire iron and rob you, or that you'd feel if you were swimming in the ocean and got caught in a riptide. I am describing the fear you choose to have when you're always worried that somebody is going to rob you, or when you believe that your life is an accident waiting to happen. In a participatory universe, many people choose to invite the consequences of fear by putting energy into being a victim or choosing a path that might invite accidents.

The kind of fear I'm referring to is an ongoing, strategic response to life. It's a chronically ingrained negative mind-set that always looks at what is likely to go wrong and all the reasons why good results are not going to happen. In a self-aware universe, there's no right or wrong, only creation. So no matter what you believe, if fear is your focus you'll make enough things go wrong and create enough disappointments that you will be convinced you're right.

Remember that life always mirrors beliefs about the self and the nature of life. Negative or disappointing results in the outer world are mirror images of counterfeit currency. If you seem to be scattering your spiritual assets like so much talcum powder on the wind instead of successfully multiplying your spiritual capital, you need to take a look at your inner world and investigate what's going on there. Under the mistaken impression that it comes from a healthy, self-protective impulse, you may be investing counterfeit currency in your life (for example: "In this industry, it's every man for himself" or "Women only want one thing from me") and feel that you're swimming upstream. Before you can truly prosper, you'll need to remove the fundamental beliefs that you created from fear-based consciousness and replace them with love.

Fear's negative approach to life and business doesn't help us respond to changing conditions, and it doesn't invite us to grow. Fear only causes us to react to perceived threats (created or imagined) and to retrench in the apparent safety of familiarity and denial. As one of my mentors, Gary Zukav, author of *Soul to Soul*, is fond of saying, the "frightened parts" of the personality show up as a feeling of inferiority or superiority, as judgmentalism, and as the feeling of being unloved and alone.[1] A better approach is to invest the loving and healthy parts of your personality in what you choose to do. This creates truly authentic power and opens up a synchronistic flow of energy that supports your efforts, fulfills you, and guides your life.

You can recognize counterfeit currency in the form of reactive inner qualities and ways of being, such as bending the truth and overworking, which you erroneously believe are necessary to attain success and fulfillment. Examples of this are the salesman who frequently exaggerates the benefits of his products to make sales (result: dissatisfied customers), and the entrepreneur who always delivers her material late because she has committed herself to too many projects and clients (result: stress and dissatisfaction). These types of fake currency pass themselves off as real and helpful, although they are not connected to the soul. Other self-protective and fearful beliefs, such as "Money is dirty, " "Life is a struggle," "Anything good doesn't last," and "Love hurts," can be deep-rooted. Your parents, teachers, and other authority figures handed down such messages to you, and others came into use during your life through social convention.

Your counterfeit currency is composed of false spiritual assets that you pass off as real. But unlike your authentic spiritual assets, which you can use to create a divinely inspired jackpot of spiritual capital, when you invest sham assets in your relationships and endeavors, you produce only diluted, ephemeral, and even negative returns. You may fool yourself into believing you're investing authentic spiritual capital, but your body will undoubtedly experience stress, such as tightness in places like your throat or solar plexus, and even create "dis-ease" that will put you in bed or the hospital.

Fear alters the formula for the generation of spiritual capital, discussed in chapter 3. Now, instead of creating pure spiritual capital, you get unrealized spiritual capital (USC), because your focus and intention are magnified by fear rather than love. If your focus were on a fear-based intention, such as the imaginary need to watch your back, we would write the formula as: $USC = (N + I + SA)^P$. In this formula, we use the letter P (from the Greek word *phobos*) to stand for fear, so as not to confuse it with F for focus. In other words, unrealized spiritual capital equals negativity plus intention plus spiritual assets, multiplied exponentially by fear.

If, for instance, you mix your spiritual capital with beliefs about the necessity of struggle, limitation, and resentment toward the powers that be, you might end up watering down your spiritual capital and making it difficult for you to have a clear focus or intentionality. You could focus on a profoundly compelling intention, such as ending hunger in your city, and no matter how hard you might try, that intention would have little or no power to materialize, because fear would keep you isolated and in self-struggle. You would mistake working hard for being effective, and worry for intentionality. Furthermore, your negative energy would push away the people best able to help you and would paralyze your network of contacts, promoting inaction and gossip.

To truly create flow and expand capital in your life, it's important to challenge your counterfeit currency and exchange it for genuine currency. Have you ever heard the phrase "The buck stops here"? Well, the "belief buck" stops with you! If someone passes on to you a fear-based belief, or one arises in your mind in response to an event in your life, your best action in that moment is to recognize the currency as the fake that it is and respond with love.

The following story is an example of the power of transforming fear-based beliefs.

JONAS'S STORY

Jonas is a middle-aged businessman who developed many of his spiritual assets, such as intuition, imagination, and the ability to empathize with people and sense their intentions, while growing up in a tough, working-class Irish neighborhood in Boston. But he attributed much of his success to a street-savvy tendency not to put too much trust in anyone or anything. He considered opportunity to be fleeting, and he believed that business — and indeed all of life — was "dog-eat-dog," which meant that he expected other people to put their own needs ahead of his. As a result, he had trouble sticking with things, and he acted in his self-interest most of the time.

When I met him, Jonas was rapidly trading stocks and flipping real estate like a short-order cook making a stack of pancakes.

Not surprisingly, his emotional life was full of dramatic ups and downs that reflected whether he had won or lost on a deal. His self-esteem rose or fell with his latest success or failure. His personal life was composed of a series of temporary relationships in which he would both consciously and unconsciously use women to satisfy his needs "before they could use him." He had some money in the bank, but he wasn't particularly happy. He wanted more from life.

When Jonas began working on his trust issues in the abundance course I was teaching at the time, among other things he found out that it was okay for him not to be "in charge." His leadership skills hardly inspired confidence; nonetheless his lack of trust had led him to believe that he had to control things and could never relax his guard. Over a period of several months, he began to see that his desire for control and his lack of trust made it difficult to attract friends who would authentically like him as a person, and romantic partners who would love him for his great spiritual assets, not simply because of what he could do, or buy, for them.

Formerly Jonas had always been quick to judge others as worthy or unworthy based on whether they had a lot of money. When he looked at these past judgments, he realized that a great many of them were not soul-based. He saw that absolutely everything he had judged as bad and had condemned in others mirrored his judgment and condemnation of himself. He also saw that his so-called winning formula of control, judgment, and noncommitment had led others to perceive him as untrustworthy, selfish, and insincere.

Jonas could be charming. He was a good listener. When money was not involved, he was kind. His authentic, love-based spiritual capital continually attracted opportunities and people to him. But his fear-based behavior limited his success because it drove away those who could help him most. Jonas's unrealized spiritual capital was a result of using his spiritual assets to pursue the negative intention of guarding against betrayal. In other words, his USC = $(N + I + SA)^P$. To transform his situation, we discussed how he needed to replace the negative focus (N) with a positive focus (F) and intensify the power of his intentions with love (L). As soon as he shifted his focus and intention to building trust, his spiritual capital immediately began to grow. It was as if the pent-up energy of good had been released. His income shot through the roof, and he soon married an authentically loving woman.

There is a bit of Jonas in all of us. Most of us have been brought up to be self-cherishing and consumed by the importance of money as a symbol of our intrinsic worth. We all wrestle to some extent with negative intentions, such as masking our feelings and controlling others, because we believe it's safer to do so. But as we become aware of our counterfeit currency, we can let it dissolve and strengthen our loving, healthy intentions, such as living with integrity and compassion and communicating genuinely.

THE MAKE-BELIEVE PAYOFFS OF COUNTERFEIT CURRENCY

When it comes to investing your spiritual capital, counterfeit currency is a nonstarter. Fear-based intentions create fear-based realities. They divert the flow of creativity into dead-end channels, where it loses power. If counterfeit currency is a significant part of your life, instead of feeling fulfillment or purpose you may be looking behind yourself at all times, afraid that one day the world will discover the terrible truth of who you really are. Most of your energy is diverted into maintaining your public image, rather than into experiencing the freedom and joy of loving creation.

So why would anyone use counterfeit currency? For the illusion of what it has to offer. If you're stuck in pain and struggle, and you're clinging to counterfeit beliefs, no doubt you're attracted to an imaginary payoff. The following is a list of signs that you're living in the land of make-believe, and some explanations of why.

- Unwillingness to change (the illusion of safety). In a creative universe, the only certainty is change. Inertia and lack of movement are signs that we fear change and are seeking safety in the status quo. When there are good things in our lives, or when we feel we've figured out how to survive and don't want to take a risk, we may attempt to maintain the status quo rather than trusting that good continues to evolve into even more good. Sadly, fearing that the unknown produces "bad" things is a self-fulfilling prophecy. To resist change is to resist Spirit.

- Addiction (the illusion of fulfillment). Going after a temporary fix or high from alcohol, drugs, or tobacco is to seek fulfillment from outer sources rather than from your soul. Besides abusing mood-altering substances, you may be engaging in any of numerous socially acceptable behaviors that are similar to those of addicts. For example, you may be unable or unwilling to stop engaging in dishonesty, denial, obsession, and so forth. Some people are addicted to sex or food. Others are addicted to attending workshops or watching TV. You may find you're addicted to seeking approval at work, in social situations, and at home — and even from strangers you pass on the street or meet while standing in line at the post office.

- Finding the negative in every situation (the illusion of control). Pessimism masks itself as concern, realism, being analytical, and so forth. It's a mind-set of separation, distrust, and powerlessness. The payoff of pessimism is being "right" in your belief that good can't last and that every apparently good situation contains flaws that make it bad. Those whose creativity is stunted or blocked are often great pessimists. Pessimism keeps you in struggle, rather than helping you overcome challenge.

- Holding grudges and hurts (the illusion of love). Within each of us there is a cry for love. But often the cry is muted. It can feel more socially acceptable to ask for love if you act as a martyr or a victim. Martyrs suffer in silence. Victims evoke sympathy by repeatedly telling their stories. In either case, the love that comes from concern is never truly satisfying. The promise of love, though tantalizing, is an illusory reward for being perpetually wounded.

- Worry about self or others (the illusion of separation). When you're in a self-cherishment mode, your focus tends to be on how the outer material world is affecting you. This permits you to fall into the trap of forgetting that you're one with the universe. To change your focus, you must realize that it's more stressful to focus on what the world does to you than on how you create your world. It's only a subtle shift to see Spirit as within you, rather than as a set of human-made rules preventing you from truly recognizing your spiritual nature. Focusing your energy on worry only creates more of what you don't choose to have.

THE SEVEN DEADLY COUNTERFEIT BELIEFS

If you desire to increase the flow of prosperity in your life, it's important to remember that there are three levels of consciousness at which you may access the field of intentionality: self-cherishing

consciousness, connection consciousness, and seva consciousness. Seva is a more potent and creative level of consciousness than
the other two, because it's an enlightened state of being in full
allegiance with Spirit. Cherishing the self puts us in the most
fearful state of being, as it is the furthest removed from recognition of oneness with Spirit.

When any of us feel we are separated from Spirit and one another, even for a short stretch of time, we tend to become self-
cherishing out of the fear of scarcity, loss, and deprivation that this
idea generates in us. Think back to the questions at the beginning
of the chapter. If you "lost" a hundred dollars by being passed a
counterfeit bill, would you feel deprived? Victimized? Would this
event signify that you were unsafe or out of control? Fear, isola-
tion, and limitation are a package.

The following counterfeit beliefs, which occur at the level of
self-cherishing consciousness, are the most damaging and un-
productive messages that underscore and run our lives. Your task
is to heal these beliefs with love. Love is all around you.

1. "I am not worthy of receiving." The idea that you deserve
   love and support only when you've done something particular to merit it is the deadliest counterfeit belief. Once
   you connect to the greater you, you see love and support
   as a birthright. When you're in selfless service, you give only
   to receive the even greater gifts of purpose, satisfaction, and
   prosperity for all. You're aware you could never outgive
   Spirit.

2. "I need to be punished." You feel you don't deserve love
   until after you have really suffered. You can dissolve this
   belief through the simple acknowledgment that you share
   the universal human need to be loved. Once you connect
   with the greater you, you perceive setbacks as blessings that

guide and enrich your path. When you're in selfless service, all is love. You're aware that by taking the path of giving, you may replace pain and suffering with harmony and oneness with Spirit.

3. "I can succeed only if I really put a lot of effort into this." It's easy to believe that nothing good is gained except by hard work and struggle. Character is often defined by a person's ability to prevail over dire circumstances. The world's greatest literature has been built upon stories of struggle and triumph. The Olympic credo specifically celebrates "the nobility of struggle." Once you connect with the greater you, however, you can easily see this belief as counterfeit. You know from firsthand experience that it's the natural state of spiritual flow for things to come into being with intentionality. Flow isn't about working harder or doing more, it's about eliminating barriers that keep you stuck.

4. "Nothing I do is good enough." You may feel as though you do your best and, even so, never get approval from your parents or from that special someone whose approval really matters to you. Challenge this by reminding yourself that you have a treasure chest of divine gifts inside you that are extraordinary and distinctive. Once you connect with the greater you, you'll perceive that, when you value yourself, the world values you. When you approve of yourself, the world approves of you.

5. "The world — even God — is against me." Self-cherishing consciousness is outwardly focused, so trust and faith are conditional at best. You believe that the conditions in your life are not your "fault" or creation. You feel that blame must be placed on someone, that others don't like you and thus are keeping you from succeeding, and that

all the power to change, create, and love is outside of you. When you accept and recognize that Spirit is working for you, and you choose to take the chip off your shoulder and know that you're fully supported in creating the world you choose, you easily elevate your consciousness to the level of connection or service.

6. "My circumstances are a result of bad karma from a previous life." In English, the Sanskrit word *karma* translates as "deed" or "action." Eastern religions that embrace the concept of reincarnation believe actions in a prior life can cause energetic effects in the current one. If you have the notion that you must suffer to pay a karmic debt, you may challenge this belief by knowing that love is the soul's currency with which all debts are paid. Karma is transmuted by joy. Above all, observe the actions (or inactions) you take to create your world. If you look closely, you'll find that what you have attributed to previous lives is actually the result of choices you've made. Embracing the idea of being your life's creator means you have the power to change.

7. "My spiritual assets aren't valuable, no matter what Ernie (or anyone else) says." There's a fearful voice inside you that wants you to believe you're the exception to the rules of Spirit, because your survival instincts insist that it's dangerous to believe you're not separate. "You have a body! You must be separate! If you think otherwise, your body could die!" it informs you. This is a sign of spiritual bankruptcy leading to extreme survival consciousness. You have incurred a deficit on the soul currency balance sheet, for which the remedy is love. Offer yourself as much love as you can on a daily basis until you know your true value.

THE GIFT OF NEGATIVITY

An interesting phenomenon occurs when people start appraising their spiritual assets and purposefully connecting with the field of intentionality: suddenly a lot of oppositional thoughts and feelings arise. Have you ever caught this happening in your own mind and body? As soon as you set an intention, do you hear a collection of negative voices in your head reminding you of all sorts of reasons you can't succeed or shouldn't try? Do terrible feelings come up to stop you in your tracks? Certain frames of mind, such as guilt, shame, and self-loathing, are liabilities you wouldn't dream of passing around as currency. You most likely want to hide these feelings from the world. Even so, they reveal your belief that you don't deserve happiness, love, success, or forgiveness. Until you understand these liabilities as the gift they are, they'll hinder your success and keep you in a perpetual state of unhappiness and endless "bad days."

Low self-esteem is a liability that frequently bubbles to the surface through self-sabotaging actions. Habitually being late, not keeping agreements, and creating excuses are the symptoms of self-sabotage masquerading as "Everything is all right." In business, this type of behavior tends to be viewed as a sign of someone who is very busy creating, which is a good thing — right? Sure, occasionally this is the case. More often it's a sign of the perpetrator's underlying belief that he or she deserves to succeed only after overcoming challenges and other conditions. It is the sign of an absence of self-love and a feeling of connection.

For instance, Claire, a private yoga instructor, was chronically tardy. She wanted to keep her agreements but often couldn't. She wasn't only a little late, but could be up to an hour late. And she always arrived stressed, even if she'd just finished teaching yoga. She habitually sped in her car. One New Year's Day, after breaking up with a boyfriend, she finally made the decision that she *deserved* to have a more harmonious life. She realized that the most important agreements that she'd failed to honor were her agreements with herself. When she finally became aware of this, she started arriving on time. She made a point of relaxing in her car on the way to her appointments by driving at the speed limit instead of racing around. By acknowledging her worth and showing herself love and respect, she found that low self-esteem stopped infecting her choices.

In one of my abundance classes, Sara, a young, recently divorced woman, seemed to be such a caring and gentle soul that many of her classmates confided in her. But Sara (like many of us) had deep worthiness issues. Although she demonstrated kindness to others, she was not kind to herself. During the safety of a guided meditation one day, she started to sob uncontrollably when she saw that her major stumbling block was how she had been unwilling to forgive herself for her divorce or to confront her guilt about how it was affecting her children.

The brilliance of Spirit is that even negativity and painful feelings serve us. They are a cry for love, a reminder to let the light of Spirit shine inwardly to reconnect with our highest nature and see the wholeness, the worthiness, the divinity, and the magnificence of who we are. When we perceive that Spirit is within us, then what is there not to love?

PAYING DOWN YOUR SPIRITUAL DEBT TO YOURSELF

In the world of finance, net worth equals the difference between what we own (assets) and what we owe (liabilities). In soul currency, value is a more fluid measurement. Self-worth is determined by what we subjectively believe we own and owe. Liabilities

— our spiritual debts to ourselves — are by-products of our self-critical thoughts, and they can be recognized as variations on the theme of being unloved, undeserving of happiness, and unworthy of ever being loved. These harsh judgments live within us and are so destructive that, for our own good, we must challenge them as soon as we perceive them, otherwise they're reflected in our lives.

You lack nothing on a spiritual level, and therefore — despite what your inner belief system may inform you — you don't have to struggle to be enough, or to do enough, or to know enough to live a financially and emotionally rewarding life. Nonetheless, your financial situation may be an example of a phenomenon that I call "roller-coaster prosperity." As if you were riding the steep ups and downs of a roller coaster, you may experience upturns (cycles of abundantly flowing money and opportunity) followed by downturns (cycles of scarcity), even to the point where the flow appears to dry up completely. The more counterfeit currency you pass around in your relationships and business, the more your reality will encompass roller-coaster prosperity.

Richard, an accomplished caterer and food photographer, blamed his constant ups and downs on feeling that he didn't deserve better, although it looked like his spending habits were more responsible for his current prosperity crisis. His lack of self-esteem was revealed through a set of self-destructive habits that showed up whenever he was about to have a breakthrough in his career. At one point, he was facing many uncomfortable circumstances. For example, his dog was dying, his business partner was moonlighting on his own, his neighbor was usurping his parking space, and his back was killing him. These conditions created a period of deep crisis in his life. To feel better, he would go shopping. When he came to see me for counseling, he was miserable and concerned that he would have to sell his condominium because the maintenance fees were too expensive.

I asked Richard what he was willing to give up to have more prosperity in his life. He answered "almost anything," and then he held his breath, half expecting I might recommend he sell his condo (which he didn't want to do). Instead I recommended we do a burning bowl ceremony right there in the office. In this ritual, we would first say a prayer and then release the ideas of victimhood, of martyrdom, and the need for approval, by writing down what he had chosen to release and then releasing it symbolically by burning it.

Next I suggested he create a "dream team" of supportive individuals (they could be alive or dead) for healing and empowerment, into which he ultimately drafted the energy of one of his favorite high school teachers, a Catholic saint, and his deceased father, who had been his biggest supporter. Whenever he felt down or alone, or created circumstances that seemed beyond his control, his job from then on would be to draw on the energy of his dream team by affirming, "I am fully loved, and I approve and love myself. I receive only good in my life."

I saw Richard several weeks later. His business, which he thought had died, had burst back into life. Money was flowing in his life once again, but this time, he put 10 percent of any money he made into a savings account, which symbolically he called his spiritual-capital seed account. He began consolidating his debts and, when I last saw him, was about two years away from being debt free. He also began making peace with his two estranged children by holding them in a vision of love. Richard and his children soon planned to spend their first Thanksgiving together in more than twenty-five years.

Ruth, also a student of mine, had been a secretary most of her life. With only a high school education, she had risen from the secretarial pool to become an administrative assistant. But her salary had risen only modestly over the many years she had been working. Her last employer had gone out of business. Now she was sixty-two, and she believed she might be too old to be hired for any responsible position. Her fears of not being good enough were coming to the surface.

During class, I pointed out that Ruth should change her focus from the belief that she was "too old" to the belief that she was able to "offer wisdom and experience." If she were wise and experienced, wouldn't a perceptive employer be clever to hire her in a managerial capacity? I suggested that, instead of fearing rejection and trying to downplay her age, she imagine what it would be like to get a phone call from someone hiring her. "That job is looking for you," I added.

Ruth went home and practiced seeing her age through the eyes of love. As she began to change her perception of herself, she grew more confident. A month later, she showed up in class with a new job. As the office manager of a large dental practice, not only was she responsible for hiring and managing the other office help, but she was also in charge of scheduling and patient relations. She had received a fat increase over her previous salary, and the senior partner had told her he'd hired her over twelve other people because of her "experience and maturity." It was Ruth's perfect job.

Mindy had just turned forty-eight, but looked many years older. She had gone to every personal development class on prosperity she could find during the last ten years and possessed literally thousands of lecture tapes. At the same time, her work had involved a series of temporary jobs, each paying a little bit more than minimum wage. She had immigrated to the United States from Ireland twenty-five years earlier and had put herself through junior college while working as a bartender. Then she left that line of work to become an office worker. She constantly talked about how money had been a challenge. Seven years earlier, she had filed for bankruptcy. Now she struggled to get by and fantasized about her dream job, which, ironically, was teaching spiritual prosperity.

Mindy's major issue was her inability to get along with others. She had many acquaintances, and most would have described her as arrogant, inappropriate, and needy. Yet, to meet her and really get to know her was to engage in conversation with someone bright who had a keen sense of humor. It was possible to sense her frustration and anger simmering beneath the surface. She had tried one job after another, mostly with the same results, and felt like she deserved better. She was so used to struggling that it had become a part of her life. She had managed to get by and move slightly ahead using positive qualities like amazing determination, persistence, and creativity.

Savvy self-help students such as Mindy, people who have gone to workshops for years, often experience the most challenging prosperity issues. Intellectually they know all the "right" action terms for soul work and can mouth them back to any listener: "Love yourself," "Heal your inner child," "Be what you want the world to be," and so on. But somehow, knowing all these modern psychospiritual terms is merely like pouring anesthetic over an unclean, gaping wound. Although the soul doesn't hurt (for the moment), it retains its unresolved damage. The liabilities of these students are tamped down into the deepest recesses of their hearts, waiting for a moment when these individuals can truly feel forgiveness and release them. They owe themselves a huge debt of self-acceptance.

Here's the advice I gave Mindy: Overcoming your liabilities (self-punishing attitudes, emotions, and behaviors) is an invitation to learn compassion and self-acceptance. Listening with love, speaking with love, and acting with love are ways to offset your liabilities and your spiritual assets and bring the balance sheet of your inner net worth into balance. Practice these techniques and see if they work for you.

Be especially careful to listen to your language. As noted earlier, the Bible, in Genesis 1:1, says, "In the beginning was the word..." because all words, even those you speak to yourself, powerfully influence reality. How many times have you uttered words like "You're such a klutz!" when you dropped something? When you were frustrated, you might have been even less charitable: "You are such an idiot! You never get things right!" You may be hardest on yourself when no one else is around. But when you speak such a phrase in the presence of the universe, even if you say it in jest or otherwise don't mean it, it's still a powerful declaration. Spirit knows the truth. Humor and jest often mask pain. Your reality reflects what you deeply believe and verbally declare.

Disempowerment and low self-esteem have a language of their own. When you speak to others, your language reveals that this is your state of mind. If you are speaking the language of doubt, insecurity, and struggle, your vocabulary will include the words *maybe, hope, possibly, but, perhaps, try, attempt, could, should, mostly, almost,* and *nearly.*

You also need to change the story you tell about yourself. What if there is someone who looks exactly like you, who walks like, talks like, and otherwise is a carbon copy of you? How would you feel if I told you that this "someone" is going around to all your friends and acquaintances and telling them stories about your inadequacies — out-and-out lies? Whenever this "someone" meets your friends, the story is perpetuated. Aren't you outraged? How dare someone spread those vicious lies and rumors about you! Your evil twin is your worst enemy.

That evil twin spreading stories about you is you, of course. Except you choose to call the hateful lies the truth. (The real trouble with counterfeit currency is not that other people believe it. It's that we believe it!) You tell the stories so that other people can know you, rather than trusting that, if you remain in a loving state of being, anyone can sense who you are. Why would it be okay for you to believe such untruths about you, but not okay for someone else to do so?

A tennis partner of mine, Angela, had been working as a temp for many years. She'd worked with forty to fifty different companies in the areas of computer support and administration. When I asked her why she didn't get a full-time job with one company so she could have better benefits and be paid more, she replied that she'd tried, but that every time she made an effort "something happened." She resigned herself to temping.

When I inquired further about what that "something" was, Angela told me her story of woe, which involved a large publishing company that had actually been excited about having her come in for an interview. The first time she was supposed to go, Angela didn't show up. Just as she was leaving her apartment, she saw that her car was missing and she thought it had been stolen. Actually it had been towed from the parking lot because she'd forgotten to put an updated registration sticker on her license plate. The prospective employer graciously rescheduled the interview for two days later. Angela played tennis that evening and told her friends the story of why she didn't have a car, and of not being able to show up for her interview.

The next day, Angela got her car out of the impound lot and made sure the sticker was on. She also made sure she would look professional and be fastidiously dressed for the upcoming interview. On the day of the second interview, she took out her car keys as she was getting on the elevator in her apartment building and inadvertently dropped them in the space between the elevator platform and the open floor. By the way, having ridden the elevator where this incident took place, I am sure that, if I tried twenty times to drop my keys in that spot, I couldn't do it. Yet Angela's word and belief powerfully created her reality: "Something happened." The building superintendent was nowhere to be found. The elevator people had to be called. Angela didn't make it to the interview and — what a surprise — she didn't land the job.

But the story has a happy ending. I drove Angela to the tennis courts a week later and pointed out how joyful she looked and felt whenever she played doubles with our group. "You would have never missed an 'interview' on a tennis court," I said. "So your problems in finding full-time employment have to be the result of how you think about work." My observation made her think.

A breakthrough came when I played against Angela and hit a very soft drop shot, which landed near the net. She never even tried to reach the ball, because she thought she'd never get it. So I kept doing this whenever I had the chance. Finally, in one great burst of effort, Angela got to the ball and hit it back with a cry, "I got it!" At the end of the evening, she told me she realized that her thoughts about never being able to get a full-time job were just like her thoughts about reaching the soft drop shots I'd been hitting. Two weeks later Angela showed up for tennis and announced she had just gotten a full-time job that she was really excited about, one with benefits and decent pay.

RETIRE YOUR EXECUTIVE COMMITTEE

False beliefs and self-punishing emotions are by-products of an aspect of personality that I call "the executive committee." This is a jury of critics that you carry around in your mind and use to judge yourself. In corporations, executive committees are set up to manage day-to-day business so that key decisions can be made quickly and their implementation can be coordinated company-wide. Although you may not have done so consciously, you've set up your own committee just like a chief executive officer would and tasked it with making decisions about your life and conduct.

Chances are that internalized versions of one or both of your parents sit on your committee, as may a teacher, a religious leader, or any other adult authority figure from your youth who was a strict disciplinarian. You might hear their voices of disapproval and judgment running on an endless audio loop in your mind. Other voices are there to remind you that you're "not being good enough," or that you're so "bad" you aren't worthy of being loved or need to be punished. Your committee dwells on all the mistakes you've made, without giving you equal credit for past successes.

Your wounded inner child lives inside your mind, too. As the noted psychologist John Bradshaw asserts in his book *Homecoming*, "When a child's development is arrested, when feelings are repressed, especially feelings of anger and hurt, a person grows up to be an adult with an angry, hurt child inside of him. This child will spontaneously contaminate the person's adult behavior. . . . Until we reclaim and champion that child, he will continue to act out."[2] Bradshaw recounts how a turning point in his life occurred when he found himself face down, drunk in a bar, at 5 AM. Drinking was his response to the rage and inadequacy he felt from still trying to win the approval of his father, who had been dead for nearly ten years.

There are two things you should know. First, you're not part of the committee in your mind, yet it's present every time you make a judgment. It has great influence over your choices and decisions in your relationships and career. Second, your soul created your committee to show you places where you feel wounded and believe that love is absent. These are places where you need to shine your light inward. Paying down spiritual debts and overcoming liabilities are not about getting love and respect from outside. They have to come from the love you give to yourself (championing the wounded you), love that the world will subsequently reflect and magnify.

Ultimately, once you realize how disempowering the invisible, but very real, committee has been for you, you can retire it permanently. Take a moment now and imagine replacing your committee, after all these years of dedicated service, with a group of supportive internal voices that empower, love, and create. Let's call this new executive committee your "dream team."

Bring in the energy of people — living or deceased — you admire and whose skills you want to emulate. Feel free to call upon the creative energy of Leonardo da Vinci or a TV character, such as the amazing problem-solving secret agent MacGyver (from the show of the same name that aired in the late 1980s), to solve challenges. Call upon the entrepreneurial mind of Apple founder Steve Jobs when you're looking for business opportunities, the writing skills of Ernest Hemingway when you set out to draft a novel, and the loving presence of Mohandas Gandhi or the Dalai Lama to resolve conflicts and make choices.

If you could include on your dream team the consciousness of anyone who has ever lived, who would you choose? Would you choose the genius of Albert Einstein, the imagination of Steven Spielberg, the wisdom of Lao-tzu, the entrepreneurship of Meg Whitman (founder of eBay), or the energy of pastor and author Joel Osteen? Make a list of the members of your dream team. Put it up, complete with photos of the members, in a prominent place. You can add or subtract members whenever you want.

DOWNSIZE YOUR FALSE BELIEFS
ABOUT SUCCESS AND MONEY

Downsizing is an effective, albeit painful, way for businesses to make a change when they experience financial challenges and operational difficulty. Downsizing is also a good metaphor for initiating personal transformation by subtracting old beliefs rather than by finding more knowledge. Let's use IBM as a case study.

Although it was one of the most successful companies of the twentieth century, in the late 1980s IBM was nearly destroyed from within by a culture of change-resistant beliefs. Among the management and the ranks, there was an inflexible adherence to a specific concept of how to be successful. For proud employees, the mystique of "the IBM way" included a dress and grooming code, a vision of lifetime security, and a central belief that the company's solution-oriented approach would command customer loyalty even if its competitors made better or cheaper products. Sadly, the IBM way of doing things led the company to be late to market with its products and to retain a bloated workforce. In an era when the most successful companies were as nimble as a pride of jaguars, IBM as an organization was acting more like a ponderous herd of elephants.

Over the years IBM's executives made some nearsighted decisions. It has long been rumored that in the 1950s IBM was offered ownership of Haloid, a small company that had developed a new photocopy technology. Haloid subsequently became Xerox, the leader in the emerging photocopier industry. Then, in the late 1970s, IBM had an opportunity to buy another innovative small company that was supplying software for desktop computers. But no matter how much Joe Sarubbi, the inventor of IBM's PC, tried to persuade his bosses, IBM's top management balked at buying Microsoft. Legend has it that a top IBM executive presumptuously said, "They'll be out of business in a couple of years." Where would IBM be today if it had made even a small investment in Microsoft?

Although it's not publicly discussed, part of the reason that IBM passed on both these companies was that neither Chester Carlson, the developer of the Xerox technology, nor Bill Gates, the cofounder of Microsoft, did things the IBM way. They did not dress or speak like IBMers. In addition, Gates was a college dropout who built his company by the seat of his pants rather than through the studied processes admired at IBM. To IBM management, his software venture seemed risky and unstable. The mythology about who they were made them resistant to change, limited their decision-making processes about what was viable, and kept them stuck in a course of pursuing traditional ventures then on the downswing, such as the data service bureau industry. This mind-set ultimately affected profits and nearly led to IBM's dissolution.

Finally, in 1993, with IBM's stock price hitting new lows, in a move that was almost unheard of for a company that prided itself on promoting from within, IBM's board of directors brought in outsider Louis Gerstner as chief executive officer. Gerstner had turned R. J. Reynolds into the powerhouse RJR Nabisco, and although he had little experience in selling computer systems, he had a lot of experience in creating lean and powerful businesses. Rather than splitting the company's divisions and selling them off, which IBM executives had been considering, Gerstner kept the company together but downsized it. Plants were closed. Nearly a hundred thousand people were trimmed from the workforce through attrition, early retirement, or divestiture of subsidiaries. As a result of those changes, IBM underwent one of the most remarkable turnarounds ever.

Like Louis Gerstner, you can make the decision to downsize: you can trim away the many beliefs that interfere with your purpose, abundance, and love. You may not have to deal with hundreds of departments employing thousands of people, as IBM did; still, identifying and "laying off" the many unhealed beliefs that you let run your life could seem equally daunting to you.

One pain-inducing myth that I held on to for years was my ego-driven belief that, while others might crumble under pressure, I was always at my best under pressure and when faced with nearly impossible timetables. This was nothing more than a cover story for me procrastinating until the last minute and not having the discipline to undertake my projects when I could do them in a relaxed and orderly fashion. I would inevitably overpromise. I would let things go until the last minute, then muster enormous effort and get the job done.

It was only after doing this for years that I recognized I had been creating these stressful situations to support my personal myth of always coming through in the clutch like a hero. I created many near misses that could have been disastrous in my investment banking career and in the many business enterprises I managed. Because I believed in and created struggle, I set myself up again and again to be under great pressure so my ego could say, "See, I did it!"

People commonly mistake struggle for the nobility of rising to meet a challenge. But there is a distinct difference. While wrestling with our challenges, we may feel at times like we're struggling; in taking on any real challenge, we gain energy that is expansive and life-giving. Overcoming a challenge transforms us and rewards us with a sense of accomplishment. Struggle drains energy because it's pointless. It robs us of life-giving purpose. Struggle feels like drowning or spinning our wheels in deep mud.

Two of my students from several years ago are fine examples of this distinction. Both Marsha and Bonnie were in low-paying service jobs that they viewed as temporary. Marsha was a restaurant hostess who went to school nights and weekends at a local community college to finish a degree in marketing. She seemed to be struggling with her two jobs, and often had to skip a semester when she didn't have the money to pay for classes. Her proudest moment was when she graduated. With her degree, she quickly got a job at a major newspaper selling advertising. She eventually moved to Pittsburgh and found employment in the marketing department of an airline company.

Bonnie, who was waiting tables in a hotel restaurant when we first met, was a complainer. She often got into unpleasant arguments with co-workers and occasionally with customers. She talked incessantly of quitting and finding a "really good" job, but instead moved from restaurant to restaurant and kept the same type of job. Although she was intelligent, she had difficulty translating concepts of empowerment into genuine empowerment of the heart. During the entire time she took classes from me, she seemed mired in relationships and jobs and struggled to make ends meet. Over the years, only the names in her various stories changed.

Your true nobility lies in diligently overcoming your challenges, as Marsha did. Challenge is the soul's call to bring out your deepest spiritual assets and put them to work. Struggle taps into your liabilities and counterfeit currency. It keeps you stuck in fear, unwilling to move forward, or prompts you to take steps backward. The process of meeting challenges, on the other hand, requires you to find renewed courage and fresh creativity when you may think you've already reached your limit. Challenge is the triumph of the soul. It fashions the sword of your character like the finest steel forged in the hottest flame. Struggle, at best, is a series of small victories for the ego. Struggle focuses on the flame rather than on the malleable steel.

There is inspiration all around us for how we may rise to meet our personal challenges. An armless man in Florida owns a landscaping business, handles a chain saw with his feet, and regularly loads and drives a truck. Another armless man is a musician. He inspires people with the beautiful music he creates by playing a guitar with his teeth and feet. If these two men can overcome their mutual challenge to build successful careers and generate income, what fearful beliefs must they have downsized to do so?

In God we trust. These words are printed on every piece of currency that changes hands in the United States. However, it's ironic that the emotions attached to money — our favorite symbol of value — lead to more distrust, discord, and dishonesty than any other tool we use. From the time you were a child, you've heard messages about money (for example, "money's hard to get," it "needs to be earned," "there's never enough," and you've got to "save it for a rainy day"). Instead of trusting that Spirit is the true source of all supply, money is used to affirm separation and limitation.

Perhaps you were brought up to trust conditionally. In general you trust that a plane will get off the ground, although there's always a shred of doubt that arises as the two-hundred-ton cylinder of metal with wings attached to it that you're sitting in lumbers down the runway. You trust that drivers coming from the opposite direction on a two-lane highway will stay in their own lanes, but you're often wary. You were warned as a child not to trust strangers, and warned not to believe everything you hear — and you don't. If you're like many other people, you firmly believe that, if you want something done right, you can't trust others but must do it yourself.

If you learned to trust life conditionally, then you also have conditional trust in Spirit. Paradoxically, you may accept the notion of a benevolent creative Spirit and mistrust the things it

has created. But how is it possible, you may ask, to trust uncon-
ditionally? Clearly there are people and circumstances that can't
be trusted? You've seen that people in your life shade the truth,
and to you this is evidence that it's worthwhile to hang on to your
mistrust.

I invite you to downsize this belief. Remember, your inner
beliefs are mirrored by reality. If you trust, you will attract and
create trust. If you have conditional trust, some people in your
life will be trustworthy and some won't. And if you don't trust
anything or anyone, your world will be filled with people who
don't trust you!

How many other mythical stories do we deal with? From
being the last one picked in childhood games, we learn the message "Nobody wants me." If our parents got divorced, we learned
the message "Everybody we love leaves," and so our own adult relationships end badly as a result. As long as we look for meaning
outside ourselves in events that we decide are meaningful, we'll
find it difficult to shift our perspective to oneness.

Endeavor from now on to see oneness in all your personal interactions and everything you do. In your spiritual practices, envision Spirit within you, expressing itself as you and melding that
self with the Creator. Oneness is the expression of loving trust, of
living in faith, and knowing that the invisible hand of the Creator opens doors at just the right time.

THE GOLD STANDARD:
BEING OPEN TO RECEIVE

Most people have more trouble receiving than giving. True
giving without conditions opens your heart. True receiving
requires your heart to already be open. When you receive a
compliment, do you say a heartfelt "thank you," or do you deflect

the compliment with offhanded remarks like, "Not really"? If you push compliments away, that inability to receive without conditions most likely shows up throughout your careers, in your businesses, and in your relationships.

In your life, the inability to generously receive might mean taking an entry-level job even when you're qualified for better work. In your business practices, it might take the form of sending bills out late and not monitoring customers who send in payments as late as possible. In your relationships, it might show up as an unwillingness to be open to empowering and loving relationships, and choosing instead to stay in a series of unhealthy, codependent relationships. Rather than see your actions as others might see them, if you're like many people with receiving issues, you might spend more time giving so you don't have to deal with the problem. It's socially acceptable to be a giving person. Even the Bible says, "It is more blessed to give than to receive" (Acts 20:35).

Giving may be Spirit's way of opening up a clear path for good to flow back to you. But if you have receiving issues, doesn't your inability to receive also hamper your ability to give? Most people have trouble receiving because they circulate counterfeit currency in the form of lack and limitation and, as a result, develop self-cherishing consciousness. If you are caught up in "Scare City" syndrome, you allow yourself to receive only when you get desperate enough to pray or when the right conditions are met. Nonetheless, the source energy of love is flowing about you.

Scientists have recently begun to find evidence that we may be genetically hardwired to be kind and generous. In other words, at birth we are all generous. In general, when we are hobbled by lack and limitation, fear takes over and this natural generosity dries up. We become prisoners of fear and the perceived need to survive.

Giving and receiving are two sides of the same spinning coin. They describe the energy of circulation and flow. When one side of the coin is pressed flat on a table, circulation is interrupted. Your first reaction may be to look only at the external circumstances, which typically show up as delays, receiving less than you expected, and the disappearance of opportunity. A woman requested me to pray that her home (which had been sitting on the market for more than nine months) would sell at a good price. After listening to her story, I told her I would pray for her heart to open and receive the flow of good.

"What about the house?" she demanded. I told her that "good" was much more than just her house. I asked her to visualize Spirit flowing abundantly through her body and filling her up with love and abundance. A week later, she had two offers on the home and sold it. She also had an unexpected job offer, at a salary 35 percent higher than what she had been making previously.

CONVERTING COUNTERFEIT CURRENCY INTO SPIRITUAL CAPITAL

Changing your thinking takes awareness, because negativity is deeply ingrained. But it's possible to convert counterfeit currency into spiritual capital. Here's how. Begin each day by resolving to be an advocate for your strengths and dreams. Do this conscientiously without allowing judgment from your committee. At every opportunity, when your subconscious wants to lapse into lack and limitation, write down what you have to be thankful for. In the beginning, do this every hour, even if you're not actively thinking about your beliefs about lack or limitation. After a few days, you'll begin to notice change.

You'll be noticeably happier and more peaceful, because you'll be connected to your "greater self," which is focused not simply on you but on all of life. Your thoughts of gratitude will gradually shift to being rather than having. Your horizon will change, from the view right in front of you, to a view with a broader, distinctly nonmaterial connection to the creative flow of love. This is the expression of you as both the creator and the participant.

Soon you will become aware whenever you lapse back into a negative focus on limitation, judgment, and unworthiness. If you're fantasizing about a negative outcome, immediately stop and change the thought by giving it a positive outcome. If you're awaiting an important yes or no decision, focus on a yes outcome rather than thinking of all the possible reasons why you could be turned down. If you look at something in a store window and your first reaction is, "I can't afford this," change the thought to: "I create the prosperity needed to buy this and more."

By shifting your view of the world, you also shift your stories from "what happened to me" to "what I am creating." The more vividly you can envision yourself as the prosperous and positive creator you are, the more powerful your intentions will be. When your stories change from being those of the victim to those of the creator, your positive thoughts will have become second nature. Share your stories with the intention that others can be inspired by them, rather than making them into arguments for your limitations. Catch yourself the moment you start on one of your old stories. Remember, no one ever built a monument to a pessimist.

Perhaps you grew up believing in some form of the adage "Hope for the best, expect the worst, and take what comes." After reading and reflecting upon the material in this chapter, you have the opportunity to transform this limiting belief and embrace a new, brighter guiding principle: "Envision love as an unstoppable force that creates great outcomes, be unattached to how your results look, and see only good."

EXERCISES FOR YOUR SOUL

The following three exercises will assist you in eliminating your counterfeit currency.

MANAGING YOUR SPIRITUAL PORTFOLIO

What Does It Feel Like When...?

For one day, fill half your wallet with Monopoly money or play money you've purchased in a toy store. On each bill, write one counterfeit belief. Then, throughout the day, as you open your wallet to make various purchases, notice your feelings at seeing the counterfeit currency all mixed up with your real cash. What if the counterfeits are so good that it's difficult to tell them from the real thing? Were you surprised when you saw the play money? Did you forget it was there? Were you embarrassed when others saw that your money wasn't real? Write down your feelings at the end of the day.

PERSONAL EXPERIENCE

The Counterfeit Currency Converter

On a piece of paper, list three of the biggest counterfeit beliefs present in the stories you tell others about yourself. Example: "I am not worthy to receive good." Leave blank spaces between each statement for the following part of this activity.

Then on a line below each statement, write an affirmation that spins this belief around 180 degrees, converting it into a spiritual asset instead of a spiritual liability. Example: "I have always been worthy, and I am open to receive good." From now on, any time your committee of critics speaks up to criticize you, you'll be prepared to challenge it with the affirmation.

MEDITATION

Retire Your Unworthiness

The most hard-core of our beliefs, such as a sense of unworthiness or a need to struggle, are often such a permanent part of our being that it's difficult to let them go. These beliefs are like addictions and illnesses; they are not simple beliefs that can be repatterned through determination. Although they represent your separation from Spirit, they have their roots deep in your psyche. You must treat these beliefs with respect and firmness, just as a company would treat a key executive whose time had come to leave the company.

Sit quietly in a comfortable position. Close your eyes and breathe easily. In a meditative state, create a ritual where the elder statesman or founder of a company has been asked to retire and leave the premises. This character symbolizes your feelings of unworthiness. Now allow yourself to feel the knowledge that, for example, the issue of struggle has been given a severance package. The intention is to honor the belief for the good things it has contributed to your life. At the same time, this belief is being retired and no longer has power over your life, unless you invite it back. To finish, draw the energy of respect into your heart.

ADVENTUREPRISE

5

The Adventure of Life and the Enterprise of Your Soul

Find your passion and connect with it, whether or not it brings you money. Ultimately it will lead to the full experience of what you were born to give.

— DONNA LEBLANC, spiritual psychotherapist and author of *The Passion Principle*

Every Christmas for more than fifty years, dreams have come to life at Lincoln Center in New York City as the New York City Ballet performs Tchaikovsky's famous ballet *The Nutcracker*, choreographed by George Balanchine. In this ballet, the young heroine, Clara, receives a special Christmas gift from her godfather — a nutcracker in the form of a soldier. But her present is broken by her jealous brother, and this sends her to bed crying. Unbeknownst to Clara, her godfather repairs the gift that evening after the house is quiet. Miraculously, at midnight all the toys come alive, and to the joy of Clara, awakened in the night, the nutcracker is transformed into an impressive soldier. But her fears also come to life, in the form of mice who scare and threaten her. The nutcracker soldier and his regiment protect Clara against the Mouse King and his minions. After the mice are driven away, lo and behold, the soldier becomes a handsome human prince who sweeps Clara off to an enchanted world of wonderment, joy, and beauty.

Is the story merely a child's fantasy? Does the miraculous happen only in stories? Or does the story symbolize our need to dream about what brings us happiness, love, and a life of fulfillment? Life calls us to dream, and when we invest our spiritual capital by taking action, our dreams actually do come alive in ways we might never imagine.

The late Reginald Lewis, an African American attorney who represented numerous clients with small businesses in New York City in the 1970s, had his offices in the Wall Street financial district, where he became a mentor and friend to me. He was a social activist as well as a lawyer, and his law practice convinced him that only when African Americans had economic power would there truly be equality. This was his dream, and little did he know then that the dream would come alive and begin to dream him.

Having spent more than fifteen years as an attorney helping hundreds of clients with financing transactions, he decided to go into the private equity investment business himself. In 1983, Lewis moved uptown and formed the TLC Group, which then bought the McCall Pattern Company, the second-largest maker of home sewing patterns, for $1 million. He discovered his own genius by following the very advice he'd given clients like me. He turned the company into an enormously profitable one that, within a few years, would be sold for about $90 million.

Spurred by his success, Reginald dreamed even bigger. When he learned that Beatrice Foods was selling off its international division in 1987, he put together the finances to buy it and then sold off parts of the company to pay down the debt from the acquisition so the company could become profitable. The resulting creation was the largest African American–owned company in history. The company's various divisions included snack food manufacturers, beverage makers, a grocery store chain, and more, with total annual sales of more than $1.6 billion.

Our dreams may be stimulated by something we see, as happened to Dan Carlson, inventor of the Sonic Bloom system. Or they may be kindled by something we're drawn to, as happened to programmer Chris Chu, who developed video games. Or our dreams may bloom in response to something that inspires us, as happened to the legendary naturalist and activist John Muir, who saved the Yosemite Valley and other wilderness areas for posterity, helping to transform them into national parks that we enjoy today. Or circumstances could prompt us to become more, show up, and play bigger, as has been the case for people such as Helen Keller, who inspired millions because she never let being blind or deaf stop her from experiencing the richness of life, or opera singer Paul Potts, a mobile phone salesman who took a chance to display his amazing voice on the United Kingdom's TV talent show *Britain's Got Talent*.

When we invest in our dreams, no matter how big or small they are, it is just a starting point. As we invest our spiritual capital, not only does the universe support us, but also the dream itself begins to dream us, taking on a richness of possibility that we might never have expected.

WHAT IS ADVENTUREPRISE?

Adventureprise is the path of connection that links your inner being with what you do. Throughout every experience in your life, your soul guides you to expand your consciousness so that you may see how much and where you are connected. It gently urges you in every moment to express your unique gifts and make a contribution. When you freely express these gifts with love and gratitude, you open yourself to accept true happiness, fulfillment, and rewards that will astonish you.

Your entire life's journey is a continuous opportunity to invest your spiritual capital and develop higher awareness as your connection with your soul and your greater self produces good in the world. When undiluted by the counterfeit currency of fear, your spiritual capital has the awesome power to create an unimpeded flow of capability, imagination, social contacts, money, and pleasure.

When you intentionally express your spiritual assets in activities that serve others, you experience a deep, abiding sense of joy and fulfillment in the work you do and what you provide. Work becomes service, and to serve is to express Spirit within. As you lay aside the fears that may have been your all-too-present companions, the universe will literally reorganize itself to reflect your soulful intentions and bring them into being. Space will be made for you to learn more about your special qualities and share them with the world. What emerges is adventureprise: the adventure of life, which is also the enterprise of your soul.

Developing the collective mind-set and habits of an adventurepreneur is the fourth step in the soul currency program. You may feel in your soul a deep passion for offering your service as a teacher, musician, or tennis player. Your soul may call you to express yourself in the professions you are drawn to: children's advocacy, designing and marketing ecologically sustainable products, holding public office, grief counseling, or financial planning. Your soul may express itself in divinely inspired talents like writing, painting, and baking wedding cakes. In the moments when you engage your heart and soul to connect with and serve others using a combination of your spiritual assets, you experience a fulfillment that comes from doing more than just a good job and bringing home a paycheck. As the universe rises to support you, your role is to stay in the flow of love and have fun. This is something you can do intentionally.

MICHELLE'S STORY

The internationally known medium Michelle Whitedove, named "America's number one psychic" by Lifetime Television, spent much of her early career as a hairdresser and aesthetician.[1] She would share intuitive information with her customers as she did their hair or nails, getting great satisfaction from giving them messages of hope, caution, and inspiration about their lives and loved ones, as well as making them look good. Still she was surprised when many of her customers and their friends called her just for spiritual readings. She initially wasn't even sure what to charge, so she suggested they pay the same amount they paid to get their hair done. Eventually, when the number of customers requesting spiritual readings outnumbered the customers who wanted their hair and nails done, she finally got the message and began to do readings full-time. Since that turning point, she has reached millions of people by making appearances on television and writing books.

The action of invisible forces that gently open doors for us can be called the "self-organizing" principle of the universe. It sets into motion the richness of adventure, but it is the soul's currency of love that lifts a lofty dream or goal and gives it depth and direction. From the dreamer, you become the dream. From the visionary, you become the vision. Michelle was simply and generously sharing her natural gifts with the people around her, and the path her soul wanted her to take showed up before her.

Michelle now has crisscrossed North America lecturing and teaching. She has given readings to heads of state, including European royalty, chief executives of major corporations, and leading show-business personalities. The cash flow that she generated through her once thriving salon business has been dwarfed by the income and opportunities that she could never have planned if she'd tried to make them happen on purpose.

FROM THE ENTERPRISE OF LIFE
TO THE ENTERPRISE OF THE SOUL

The enterprise of life is constant. We normally don't use a workplace vocabulary to describe what we do in our nonworking life, yet there really is no division between career and personal life. Any perceived division is imaginary. Corruption in one area of life always spills over into other areas, and healing in one area of life always initiates healing in other areas, for the simple reason that spiritual capital is the mother of all capital. It creates whatever it is directed to create when we are open to giving and receiving. Business imitates life. Life imitates Spirit.

Here's why you can consider your life an enterprise much like a sole proprietorship or any other business venture:

- You set the same types of goals for success (although perhaps on a smaller scale) that a small business or sole proprietorship would. Financial growth and stability, a safe and satisfying home base, and a positive image and reputation are common objectives.
- You surround yourself with a supportive team of consultants, key management personnel, and volunteers (for example, a babysitter, accountant, doctor, auto mechanic, minister, and so on) who support you as you handle challenges. Your life is filled with stakeholders, people who benefit from your success, just as a company is.
- You make command choices for your life, like any successful chief executive would, and override choices made for you that don't appeal to you.

- At times, you marshal your inner and outer resources as well as Bill Gates or Steve Jobs. For example, you learn to deal with unpleasant news or setbacks. You figure out creative ways to get what you want. A single mom who has moved her family into a new apartment and can't afford furniture would make any entrepreneur proud as she reaches out to friends, visits thrift shops, and checks neighborhood bulletin boards to meet her challenge.
- You create a culture in your life, such as a culture of creativity, fun, or inertia, in the same way that every organization creates a collective culture. Companies proudly announce their cultures of innovation, promotion from within, and social action. Some have inbred cultures in which outside ideas and innovations are not welcome, or that use fear tactics to spur greater performance.

There are differences between the enterprise of a life lived on a self-cherishment level, and the adventureprise of a life lived on the level of connection or — among rare individuals — in seva. In all types of life, you can be successful and financially rewarded. However, the enterprise of a life run by counterfeit currency can only be temporarily gratifying. It doesn't bring you real, lasting soul fulfillment, which is a result of love being activated. In the enterprise of life, your focus shifts from event to event. Adventureprise exists when you wake up and connect the dots between different events and different areas of life.

Ironically, if your primary goal in reading this book is to be paid better, you will be interested to know that, after you develop success and gain money, things, and some satisfaction about that success, your greatest sense of fulfillment will come about if you give your money and things away for a higher purpose. You'll reach this understanding on your own after you reveal and reduce the influence of the counterfeit currency in your life.

Adventureprise, which is the material version of the soul's path, is so attractive that it seems always to be gently inviting us to grow and become more.

THE EMERGENCE OF FULFILLMENT

Take a look at your own life. Are you fulfilled in what you do for a living? When you wake up in the morning, does what you do make you look forward to the day? Or have you settled for a job that could probably pay better, be more enjoyable, and be a lot more fulfilling? Do you tell yourself, "Someday, I'll find something to do that I really love"?

Are you playing it safe? After all, you have the mortgage, car payments, and other expenses to pay. Most people will cling to a job until it becomes so intolerable or insecure that they're forced to leave. At some point, you may have decided you would take enjoyment from your personal life, rather than your career; that fulfillment is desirable but not mandatory; and that maintaining a certain income is preferable to going out on a limb in order to earn more money. If you've changed your mind and you now want it all — pleasure in your work, soul fulfillment, and higher income — your soul is calling out to you to learn the lessons of connection and service.

People most often seek a way out of financial trouble by becoming entrepreneurs. Even though more than 80 percent of small businesses fail in the first five years, as business visionary and author Michael Gerber points out in *The E-Myth Revisited*, wanting to be your own boss and build a company that makes millions is the stuff of urban legend. Ask any entrepreneur who has put in fourteen-hour days in a startup what it's like to live and breathe an enterprise. As one told me, "It's like doing time."

People may think they have become entrepreneurs to make

money, but really their business is a microcosm of life in which they're working out their spiritual issues. Self-employment is one of the greatest laboratories for working out beliefs about trust, worthiness, and receiving. If you start a business, as early as the first week you'll attract circumstances to heal unhealed anger, negative judgment, and low self-esteem, and you'll continue to attract similar circumstances until you elevate your consciousness. For example, if you have issues related to trust, you'll communicate distrust to those around you. You'll create situations that show you that you can't trust anyone. You'll habitually second-guess yourself. When you have conditional trust in life, then you separate yourself from Spirit within you by choosing to have limited trust in Spirit's ability to deliver. The universe will be a mirror of your fear.

Before raising capital for someone new, my investment bank always did its due diligence, which meant running extensive background and credit checks on the people and companies we were raising money for. On one occasion, a software company's chief executive made a point of telling us that he distrusted most "Wall Street people." On another occasion, he told us he distrusted companies in his own industry. Imagine our surprise when our routine background check showed that the man had had his driver's license suspended for traffic violations. Most recently he had been cited for driving with a suspended license. When confronted with this information, he denied it and said, "It must have been someone with a similar name."

Thinking perhaps he was correct, we checked again. But there was no mistake. He continued to deny it, and then, when confronted with a copy of the court record, acted surprised to discover that his license had been suspended. When our investment committee met to consider raising $5 million for this executive's software company, the first thing the head of corporate finance said was, "If he lied to us about his driving record, how truthful will he be about how he spends the money we raise for him? And if there is some bad news, we'll be the last to hear about it." In this case, the man's distrust of us created a situation in which we distrusted him. When we turned down his company, for him it was probably just one more instance of the idea that "you can't trust Wall Street."

If, in taking a look at your predominant beliefs and actions in the workplace, you recognize that your adventureprise is operating on the level of self-cherishment, the biggest shift you can make is to stop playing it safe. The act of focusing on survival and limitation prevents you from getting in touch with your passion. Focusing on the external aspects of the world robs you of the inner power you need in order to invest your spiritual capital in activities that excite you.

Perhaps you're an artist and you're doing what you love, but you don't have any cash in your pocket. Quite possibly you have limited the expression of your creativity to one dimension of your life. I've seen plenty of creative artists who needed to learn how to market themselves, pay closer attention to detail, and put more hours into developing their craft. They played it safe by choosing to be impractical dreamers and do only the things they were used to doing. To move forward and be more successful, you must invest a wide variety of spiritual assets in your adventureprise. You must diversify.

If you have cash, but you're not yet doing work you love, you may be confusing material pleasure and the far deeper fulfillment and joy that come with inwardly generated actions and feelings. Often small businesspeople work hard and settle for lack of fulfillment in exchange for bringing in money, which signifies security. To get out of this mode of limitation, it's important to test out new combinations of interests and activities you love. Do them because they feel good, and see where they lead. You may find, for example, that the half hour you spend tutoring a young child in the game of basketball might put you in touch with how satisfying it is to serve others, to challenge yourself by helping another grow through challenge, and to make a difference in your own life by making a difference in the life of another.

The spirit within is sometimes not so gentle in its urging. Often this urging takes the form of a dark night of the soul. A former tennis acquaintance of mine, a leading advertising executive, pursued a cocaine habit by night. Eventually, his marriage fell apart, his firm asked him to take a leave of absence, and he found himself living in a one-room flat deep in debt. After nearly a year of rehab, he was offered a better position at a more prestigious advertising agency, and he soon found himself a frequent guest on morning and afternoon news programs. His rehab experience motivated him to speak before many groups about drug addiction and recovery. His audiences have ranged from Boys and Girls Clubs to Madison Avenue executives at dinner meetings. And he has raised more than $3 million for various teen and adult recovery and addiction groups.

Personal development and education are spiritual assets that elevate the level of consciousness you invest in life. When you bring a greater spiritual awareness to the challenges of life, only then can you change the focus on the outer world and truly understand that, by changing the inner landscape, you change the material world around you. It may be difficult for someone who is going through a dark night of the soul to see beyond a financial or health crisis, the loss of a job, or a serious or crippling illness. But often what appear to be our greatest challenges are really wake-up calls and blessings in disguise. These are opportunities to break free of the bonds of limitation that have kept us stuck in a state of false limitation and victimhood.

When you are focused on "having," your adventureprise will reflect your inner survival issues and counterfeit currency. You're likely to experience disappointment and struggle, as well as wins and losses, depending on which of your limiting beliefs is operative. If you typically attach your self-worth to successful outcomes in your enterprises, you'll identify as good days those on which you make progress toward your goals, an opportunity opens up, or you have an unexpected victory. You'll describe as bad days those on which there are setbacks to reaching your goals, an opportunity disappears or is delayed, or you have an unexpected disappointment. Self-cherishment is a mind-set that produces highs and lows. When you focus on yourself too much, it's easy to forget that your outer world reflects your inner state of being.

Years ago when I was visiting China, I jotted down an old Chinese proverb about flow, attributed to the twelfth-century Confucian sage Zhu Xi: "You might as well try to keep the wind from blowing. When you oppose it, it goes around you and often runs you over. When you flow with it and use it, you can ride the wind to heaven." Reflect on this idea whenever you feel events are outside your control.

THE ADVENTUREPRISE OF CONNECTION WITH THE GREATER YOU

The greater you, your self that is connected to your soul, naturally gravitates toward opportunities to benefit others, such as green businesses and services and products that improve the quality of life for others. When you go into a business such as these, you expect financial gain, but your mission is more important to you than simply making money. When you intentionally connect with the greater self and the good you can do for others by making a contribution to the world, you're able to connect with your passion. When you incorporate the greater self into what you do, any duality between what you are and what you do begins to disappear. True fulfillment comes when your being and doing are connected as one.

When author Laura Duksta was eleven years old, she contracted alopecia areata, a disease that caused all her hair to fall out permanently. Ashamed of how she looked, and feeling like a freak, she wore wigs for more than nineteen years. The day she saw that she was beautiful on the inside was the day she realized that "bald is beautiful" as well. In the months and years that followed, not only did Laura begin expressing love for others in every aspect of her life, but she also opened up to receive the love that Spirit expressed as her and for her. Once she understood that love is an eternal truth not conditional upon how you look or what you do, that there is perfection even in things that seem imperfect, she changed her way of living and began making a powerful contribution.

While attending Science of Mind classes at the Center for Spiritual Living in Fort Lauderdale, Florida (where I serve as an assistant pastor), and by doing other personal development work, Laura slowly but surely realized that receiving love is a choice, and that loving yourself is just as important as loving others.[2] As she began to recover her self-love, she decided to write a children's book. She had previously never written a children's book or, for that matter, any other book. She faced long odds for getting this book out to the world.

Laura's adventureprise, which became *I Love You More*, was a miraculous journey of faith that brought her together with illustrator Karen Keesler, whose mother had cancer. Within six months the book took shape and was ready to be published. But there were no takers, especially for the book of an unproven, first-time author. This didn't stop Laura, who decided to independently publish it and promote the message "Love should be seen, heard, felt, sensed, shown, expressed, talked about — and more." Laura's message of love for children and their parents led her to visit hundreds of schools, churches, and parenting organizations. Because of its powerful theme and Laura's investment of her spiritual capital, *I Love You More* began to be placed on reading lists. To date, Laura and Karen's book has sold more than two hundred thousand copies, making it one of the top-selling children's books in the country.[3]

The success of her book, and Laura's journey around the country, has created an enormous blossoming of love, personal growth, and financial flow in her life. In this journey, Laura has found deep personal spirituality and has affected hundreds of thousands of children and adults with an inspiring message of love and self-esteem. Her screen name says it all: she is "A Bald Star." Her adventureprise and message of love continue.

For most of us, the consciousness of the greater you often gets interwoven with our self-cherishment consciousness. But the consciousness of being can never be fully realized so long as it's mixed with this lower-level consciousness of having, because it manifests as the consciousness of "having a greater connection" rather than of "being the greater connection." Consistently shifting your focus to connection is the most important choice you can make at this level.

Why is this so important? The power of spiritual capital creates the form of connection and even provides you with initial bursts of energy to garner support. However, if you don't shift your focus to connection, you won't create richness and inner fulfillment. You'll lose energy after you've created the project or organization. There may be delays in your plans, and they'll take on the characteristics of self-cherishing adventureprise — its volatility, its ups and downs.

Creating from a greater connection of being opens up the

flow of resources and a path of creation to you. True creativity is expansive and multidimensional, not just "bigger." As one of the many facets of love, receptivity is a significant aspect of your soul currency. Learning to operate from this level of consciousness for an extended time draws upon collective energy and material resources. You almost surely need social support from a peer community of like-minded individuals to do it. And you definitely require a spiritual base in your life. For if you don't believe there's anything beyond what you experience with your five senses, you'll never get to a point where you feel truly fulfilled. There's a part of you that will always feel empty and separate.

Understanding the good you give through simple connections opens you up to receiving the flow of soul currency. By seeing beyond what immediately affects you, you become able to invest your powerful spiritual capital in ways that bring you lasting fulfillment. Finding your proverbial life's passion is not just about discovering what you enjoy doing; it's also a process of developing your deep connection to the inner qualities of your Spirit, which expresses itself through you.

Sometimes finding our connection to something greater than us results from adversity. This was the case for Karen Simmons, a Canadian-born gemologist and full-time mother. After having four squirming, active children, she had a fifth child, the quiet Jonathan, who was diagnosed with autism, a disease that blocks people's ability to speak and otherwise communicate easily. She was devastated by her doctor's pronouncement that there was no cure, and that in all likelihood Jonny would end up in an institution. She was determined that, no matter what she had to do, she would not allow this to happen.

Karen went on an insatiable quest for knowledge, learning more about the disease and the latest treatments and support for autistic children. She was stunned to discover that there are millions of children with autism, and that the disease is approaching epidemic proportions, with one autistic child for every 150 American children. In some other countries, the percentage is the same or greater.[4] As a loving parent, Karen saw Jonny's gifts, his beauty, and his magic, and she focused on bringing them out. Although not a writer, she produced the first of seven books, *Little Rainman: Autism through the Eyes of a Child*, with four coauthors, so her son could understand his own autism and the people around him. In 2007 she coauthored *Chicken Soup for the Soul: Children with Special Needs: Stories of Love and Understanding for Those Who Care for Children with Disabilities* with Jack Canfield, Mark Victor Hansen, and Heather McNamara.

Karen's passion for her own son and other special needs children led her to form the KEEN (Key Enrichment of Exceptional Needs) Educational Foundation. Later, when Future Horizons, the world's largest publisher of books on autism, asked her to become their exclusive Canadian distributor, she started Exceptional Resources, now called Autism Today. Currently, the organization serves a community of more than fifty thousand families. It has grown from a simple one-computer, home-based business to an international organization that receives more than 3 million visits to its website per month.

SEVA ADVENTUREPRISE

Often when we emanate the energy of selfless giving, what is returned to us almost defies description. When we give with the intentionality of unconditional service, we create an expanding vortex of the most powerful form of the soul's currency: love. Ironically, the "returns" do not resemble most of the ways we normally measure value in our culture, such as money, status, and objects. Look at what happened to Al Gore. When he lost his bid for the

U.S. presidency, he shifted his focus to his passion for protecting the environment, and won an Academy Award for his film and the Nobel Peace Prize for his service. As a spokesperson for planetary healing, he has been rewarded with friendship, admiration, and influence, as well as financial prosperity. He also looks like he's having a lot more fun and fulfillment than he had before.

One of the greatest contemporary seva adventureprises is the life path of the Buddhist monk Tenzin Gyatso, a man also known around the world as His Holiness the fourteenth Dalai Lama. Born in Tibet, the child of simple farmers, the Dalai Lama as a young boy learned about compassion and kindness from his mother and other members of his immediate family. At four he was discovered to be the reincarnation of the thirteenth Dalai Lama and was brought to Lhasa, the capital of Tibet, to begin a life of service to his people. Historically the Dalai Lama is both the spiritual and the political leader of the Tibetan nation. While young he often would rather have been playing outdoors than studying and memorizing the Buddhist texts that were part of his training to remember the path to enlightenment. Yet he chose to study.

His Holiness has been awarded the Nobel Peace Prize, the U.S. Congressional Medal of Honor, and more than a hundred honorary doctorates and other major peace and humanitarian awards from around the world. At the Congressional Medal of Honor ceremony, it was remarked that, while still a child, the Dalai Lama had met President Franklin Roosevelt, who gave him his own gold watch. The president also gave him a replica of the Statue of Liberty, a compelling symbol of freedom for all people, which the young boy placed by his bedside. In 1959, while in his late twenties, His Holiness was forced into exile when the Chinese People's Liberation Army conquered Tibet. He has lived in exile ever since, a symbol for religious freedom and preservation of Tibetan culture. In this way, he has preached a message of tolerance, kindness, compassion, and love. When asked once what his religion was, he replied, "My religion is kindness."

The greater ideas of religious and cultural freedom, tolerance, and forgiveness are such pure truths that they have attracted support from every corner of world. Tens of millions of dollars have been donated to support the work of the Dalai Lama as a global spokesperson.

Often selfless dedication to humanity goes unrecognized until it touches someone's life directly. Sometimes it is attacked or mocked by the wider community, as it was for a spiritual healer in South America. In central Brazil, João Teixeira de Faria, a man who has become known simply as João de Deus (John of God), is a medium and healer who, by some estimates, has helped more than 14 million people in different capacities. The numbers become even more staggering if you consider that the people he directly serves are connected with friends, family, and acquaintances who benefit from the energy of their healed presence. Thus the pure force of his loving energy ripples outward tremendously. Despite opposition from local medical doctors and religious leaders, including arrests, lawsuits, beatings, and even an assassination attempt, João de Deus, along with his spiritual center, the Casa de Dom Inácio (the House of Saint Ignatius of Loyola) in Abadiânia, Brazil, has been a magnet for those seeking to be healed, often from incurable diseases, or simply to grow spiritually.[5]

The ministry of João de Deus exemplifies how love magnifies all that it touches and makes it prosper. With only a second-grade education, young João spent many years doing his healing ministry in different villages and even for a local branch of the Brazilian military. He goes into a trance, and spirit beings work through him. He takes no credit for the cures that are accomplished. "It is not I who does the healing," he insists. "It is God who intervenes through the compassionate spirits that use my body." Indeed, this medium, who has devoted nearly fifty years to hosting a group of compassionate healing spirits, remembers little or nothing of what occurs. The Casa de Dom Inácio is supported by donations. There is no charge to visit with the medium.

The once sleepy town of Abadiânia in Goiás Province, whose inhabitants formerly made bricks, has become one of the fastest-growing and most vibrant economic zones in all of Brazil. Restaurants, hotels, and even two Internet cafés have opened to accommodate travelers. Jobs have also been created at the Casa de Dom Inácio. Love has created compassion, cooperation, and kindness in the wider community, much like it has in the communities near the world's most famous spiritual centers, such as the Findhorn community in Scotland, the Lourdes shrine in France, and the Medjugorje shrine in Bosnia and Herzegovina. Americans and other visitors from nearly every country once only trickled in but now compose a majority of the visitors to Abadiânia. Yet the resources created by João de Deus are invested in some of the poorest parts of Bahia and other satellite areas where the medium travels to see tens of thousands of residents each month.

Many seva adventureprises are shaped around greater ideas of group service. Examples are: Doctors Without Borders, an international organization that helps the injured and the sick in war-torn and disease-ravaged areas; the Institute of Noetic Sciences, whose goals are the exploration of scientific knowledge for peace, healing, and increased human potential; and the Association for Global New Thought, which has connected a diverse group of people, such as the Dalai Lama, the late Yolanda King (daughter of Martin Luther King Jr.), and Arun Gandhi (grandson of Mohandas Gandhi) to promote world peace through the consciousness of peace, wholeness, and love.

Seva adventureprise is a magnet for attracting resources and stirring the souls of humankind: the greater the idea, the greater the support for it. Comedian Steve Bhaerman, known professionally as Swami Beyondananda, once wryly observed, "It took millions of dollars to keep Gandhi poor." He was, of course, referring to the massive donations that Gandhi received for doing his selfless service. The ability to give selflessly to a truly noble effort that embodies love and peace and transcends fear-based human reactions, comes from the greater self within each of us. The more we use this ability, the more we remember that one of the most important ways to experience Spirit is through service and giving.

To practice seva, let life call to you. Children are more willing to do this than most adults are. When children perceive a need, they act. For example, since 1997 more than two thousand children have donated their hair to Locks of Love, a nonprofit organization that aids children who have lost their hair from alopecia, chemotherapy, and other medical conditions.[6] They aren't yet so vested in a particular path that seva raises the fear in them that their lives will change. Children expect life to change them. With hearts and minds focused on learning and absorbing experience, they hear the call of life.

WHAT MUST I BECOME?

An immensely popular TV show in the late 1960s, *I Dream of Jeannie* featured an astronaut, Major Anthony Nelson (played by Larry Hagman), who finds a bottle on a deserted island. He brings it home and inadvertently rescues a mischievous genie (played by Barbara Eden). She becomes his slave, granting his every wish — and falls in love with him. In almost every episode, the hilarity of near-disaster follows Nelson in his home, at his workplace, and in his romantic life as a consequence of his being too vague about what he wishes for — or too literal. Sound familiar?

Hmm. Who else might not always be clear or careful when setting intentions?

In our own lives, we're like Major Nelson, and we're also like Jeannie. We cocreate the world we live in by declaring our intentions, which we reinforce when we choose where to invest our spiritual capital. When we make a loving investment of our abilities and intentions, it's as if we're uncorking a bottle inside us, from which our inner genie emerges. Like a genie, our intentionality materializes possibility. Our dominant thoughts, including our counterfeit currency and liabilities, shape the boundaries of our creation. These even define the edges of what we judge to be a success or failure. But we never know exactly what the consequences and outcomes of our intentions will be. And therefore we have to learn to trust the accidental and the unfamiliar and to go with the flow of life, rather than living in fear of catastrophe, struggle, pain, and loss.

Learning to live with the mystery of life means being willing to act as if everything that comes your way may yield the highest good for you and others. It's an optimistic approach to surprises, one that will enable you to see fresh opportunity everywhere.

So often we have a talent or enthusiasm waiting to emerge. Suddenly life "accidentally" creates the right opportunity for this spiritual asset to burst forth and be liberated like a butterfly breaking out of a cocoon. When we're persistently available, life can take unexpected turns.

My student Beatriz Ayende, a tall, beautiful woman in her late thirties, long had a hidden passion for belly dancing. A successful marketing associate for a large insurance company, she took dance classes nights and weekends. Only a handful of people at her office knew. Then her company relocated and offered her a choice of either moving to North Carolina or being laid off. After several visits to North Carolina, she decided to move there.

A week before she left, by chance she met the owner of a nearby Greek restaurant while in a local pharmacy. He stopped to say hello and, because he'd seen her dance, offered her a job as an entertainer in his restaurant. The timing of the offer was a signal Beatriz recognized as an invitation from her soul to turn in a new direction. She made up her mind to stay in South Florida and follow her passion. As a result her adventureprise has led her to open a dance school, craft a dance-fitness program for women of all ages, write articles, make instructional DVDs, and perform in cities and venues that she had never imagined visiting in her previous career.

To find your destiny, a great question to ask yourself is: "What must I become?" The path of your adventureprise will become more detailed and clearer to you with each challenge and opportunity. As your vision gets stronger, it will provide a framework through which you will receive increasing prosperity. No matter how much money you make, remember that you're creating a path that provides a sense of accomplishment. Soon you'll look back and be able to see how far you've come on your journey.

INNER AND OUTER FLOW

Being well paid to do what really fulfills you is a sign that you're immersed in soul currency, the source energy of Spirit. When you evaluate your adventureprise, remember that this path is an expression of your value. Without you, there wouldn't be a journey or the gifts you bring to the world. Regardless of what or how big the dream is, to be in harmony with the flow of soul currency is also to recognize your extraordinary value.

While you personally may know few people who exemplify the power of adventureprise, one of America's best-known talk show hosts, Oprah Winfrey, is one of them. She could not have imagined when she was growing up in Kosciusko, Mississippi, that every day she would inspire, inform, and entertain more than 30 million television viewers. Her adventureprise has expanded to include not only *The Oprah Winfrey Show* but also *Oprah's Big Give*, a reality TV show she produced about a charitable campaign; *O, the Oprah Magazine*, one of America's most successful publications; the *Oprah and Friends* radio show on Sirius Satellite Radio; the Broadway show *The Color Purple*; and a groundbreaking ten-week-long Internet video course with Eckhart Tolle that is centered on his bestselling book *A New Earth*.

What attracts her enormous daily viewing audience, as well as the unprecedented half million to a million participants in her class with Tolle, is how seriously Oprah takes her own personal development, and her joy at helping others. *Oprah's Big Give* focuses on and encourages individuals and groups who are actively giving and helping others in their community. Her compassion gives countless others permission to open their hearts.

Born to unwed teenage parents, Oprah grew up in extreme poverty on her grandmother's farm. She learned to read at three and has called books her "greatest teachers." She spent much of her childhood moving from place to place, gave birth to a premature baby who died, and ran away from home with an older boy. Her life changed when she went to live with her father, Vernon Winfrey, a barber and businessman who taught her the value of education and discipline.[7]

Oprah used her spiritual assets of personality and determination to land her first television broadcasting job, at WVOL in Nashville, Tennessee, while still in high school. At age nineteen, she became the first African American woman on the air at

WTVF-TV. Three years later she landed a job as the 6 PM news anchor at the Baltimore station WJZ-TV. Her personality and demeanor, and the spiritual capital she invested in serving others, soon won her the cohost spot on a local talk show, *People Are Talking*. Her adventureprise had already begun. Eight years later, she became the host of *A.M. Chicago*, competing opposite Phil Donahue's top-rated national talk show. A year later, her show, re-dubbed *The Oprah Winfrey Show*, became America's top-rated talk show.

Her adventure in life has lifted Oprah in directions she never dreamed she would go when she began her broadcasting career. Her adventureprise has always prospered because it's also the enterprise of her soul. As the first black female billionaire to make the *Forbes* 400 list, she is one of the few women ever to create a fortune of this magnitude instead of inheriting it. She is also one of only three women ever to own her own movie and TV studio (Mary Pickford and Lucille Ball were the others). But, as Oprah writes in the February 2008 issue of *O, the Oprah Magazine*, "I am not my money." The money is like applause for a ministry and adventureprise that is changing the world.

It's important to understand, however, that success is not about how much you have, but about allowing yourself to open up to Spirit within you to consciously create something supportive, healthy, loving, and expansive. The ideas we hold about material success and our attachments to these limiting beliefs are often the very barriers that stand in our way. You might take a job because it pays more money or is a "good career move." If so, you're putting up with the parameters of that job in exchange for the certainty of a paycheck, because you believe you'll never be as well paid doing what you love to do. In adopting this approach, you postpone doing what makes you happiest, just because your bills are being paid. The job may offer you benefits, even the opportunity to do certain things you enjoy doing. However, you avoid taking action because your fear of change may be stronger than your desire for the joy of fulfillment. It's still all about you.

If you happen to be one of the 14 percent of people who the experts say are doing what they really enjoy, you are indeed one of the fortunate. If you're not well paid yet, then there is some type of counterfeit currency in your mind that needs to be healed.

Where do I start? How do I overcome fear? How do I know I'm making the right choice? When do I quit my job? What do I do if I make a mistake? If any of these questions have popped up in your mind while you read this chapter, here are four ways to begin answering them.

Principle 1. Lead from Your Strengths

Start by loving who you are. When you do that, see how much of what you take for granted is unique. You are special, although this fact may seem difficult to swallow if kids made fun of you when you were growing up because you looked different, or teased you because your English wasn't great. I have some experience in this myself. Although I am an American by birth, I grew up in an era when there were relatively few people of Asian descent living in the United States. Many unfortunate stereotypes about Asians existed in those days, so as a child I was often teased and sometimes taunted.

Today, I see being Chinese American as a big advantage: I generally stand out in a crowded room, and when I talk about the two fields I've chosen to become an expert in (finance and spirituality), people automatically assume I know something about them because Chinese people are so successful and China has a long, great spiritual tradition. I also have a great advantage in business when I entertain people on my home turf, a good Chinese restaurant. When I quote Buddha or Lao-tzu, people think I'm wise. Even though as child I felt inadequate due to my height, today it doesn't matter that I may be a little short, because I am successful — and I'm also aware that the tallest man in the National Basketball Association, Yao Ming, is Chinese.

If you smiled because what I've said rings true, remember to cherish your own heritage. You may feel like you're an accident of birth, but remember, in the intelligent universe that we are part of, there are no accidents. For example, if you're a native Spanish speaker, you can start by envisioning opportunities or jobs where this is an advantage. You don't have to work in a Spanish-speaking neighborhood or a Hispanic-owned company, just envision Spanish as one of many tools that will widen your audience. If you're in sales or marketing, it could make you more effective in dealing with customers — or patients or students or parents, depending on the job you do. If you are older, see your experience as an advantage. If you're a woman, don't automatically assume that you're limited to a stereotyped gender role in the workplace.

Here are some areas in which you should consider your strengths:

- Heritage: Learn about your family heritage and culture. I had the advantage of learning about Chinese culture as part of my upbringing, and I studied it in depth later in my life. Rather than feeling left out because I looked different, I began to love what I was and came to see it as a divine gift. I am fortunate to have received the gifts of two great cultures: the richness of Chinese culture and the freedom, innovation, and imagination of American society.

- Ancestry: Learn about your ancestors. When I was growing up in Queens, New York, I thought little about my ancestors. All I wanted to do was fit in and be like every other kid on the block. Later I learned that my uncle had been the vice foreign minister of China, and that my paternal grandfather had been a high-ranking official under Chiang Kai-shek. A few years ago, I also learned that parts of my family tree have been traced back nearly a thousand years, to the Sung dynasty. Now this is a strength, because China is a major world power and everyone wants to know more about it.

An acquaintance of mine, Sarah Caldicott, grew up hearing at the dinner table that she was the grandniece of Thomas Edison. She has spent most of her life in branding and advertising, and a few years ago she decided to go deeper into corporate training. She made the most of her ancestry by titling the management book she coauthored *Innovate Like Edison.*

- Persona: Your persona (the way your personality is outwardly expressed) is yours alone. Your smile may be infectious. When you speak from your heart, you may be persuasive. Your directness may get people to trust you. These are signs of individual character. The eyes may be the windows to the soul, but your persona is what makes you unique. And when you love what is authentic about you, others will love you as well. When you value the persona you are expressing, then the world will value it as well. Lead from your strengths.

My good friend Maureen Whitehouse, a former international model, spokesperson, TV personality, and actress, was burned out by a life based only on exterior looks and values. Now a mystic, personal development coach, and author of *Soul-Full Eating*, she teaches that love, beauty, and value come from the inside rather than the outside of a person.

Principle 2. Invest Your Spiritual Capital

When clarity and inspiration come to you, it's Spirit's invitation to step through the doorway of opportunity, a call to action that could easily be mistaken for a passing idea. For you, the action of investing your spiritual capital might be to consider taking tiny steps so this idea can flourish and be brought to life in the illusion of the material world. Your empowerment also gives others permission to open up to their own greater selves. We all are drawn to great ideas like moths to a flame. At some level, once you hear a call from Spirit, you get the sense that a prayer has been answered or that a divine gift has been handed to you on a silver platter.

What should you do if you get a good idea? Write it down. Make a request to Spirit for the idea to be connected to an action. What do you do if it's an idea that has come as a result of your intentionality and focus? Check your intuition and follow it.

Sometimes ideas come from observing what happens around us. Velcro, for example, was invented by a Canadian engineer who, finally frustrated by the painstaking process of having to pull cockleburs out of his dog's coat, decided to look at them under a microscope.

In 1970, the 3M researcher Spencer Silver, who was trying to develop a strong adhesive, concocted a batch that easily came unstuck. Four years later, he suggested coating the bookmarks for hymnals with this "weak" glue so they wouldn't fall out but could still be removed without damaging the pages. Thus an entire industry of Post-it products was born. A colleague of Silver's, Art Fry, worked in 3M's new-products area and saw the potential for using the tacky glue for bookmarks and sticky notes. He wrote up a proposal. 3M's Post-it notes are one of its bestselling products ever.[8]

You don't have to be a scientist in a laboratory to recognize opportunity. In 1905, Frank Epperson, who is widely credited with inventing the first Popsicles, left a flavored drink with a stirring stick in it overnight on the back porch, where it froze. Nearly twenty years later, as he focused on creating a business opportunity, he applied for a patent and began to sell what he then called "Eppsicles," made in several different flavors. His children renamed it "Popsicle." Good Humor Ice Cream now owns the rights to it.[9]

The Internet search engine Yahoo (an acronym for "Yet Another Highly Officious Oracle") was developed by several college students who got together to laugh, study, and throw around outrageous ideas on how to improve search engines and establish online communities.

Whether the gift of an idea or further clarity comes to you while you're hanging out with friends, or you're in the shower (as Einstein reported happened to him), or it pops into your mind as the first thing you think about when you wake up in the morning, recognize that it's an invitation to take action. Many people take no action on their brilliant ideas and, years later, may see "their idea" become a million-dollar product sold by someone else. Others are prompted by their unborn project to develop form around it, and it becomes a company, a partnership, or a nonprofit organization. They embrace the idea.

Principle 3. Be Unattached to How It Looks

Be unattached to the form your adventureprise takes. Be attached instead to determining how you will best serve a market or need that will improve the quality of life for everyone. Be attached to the greater mission of what you do. Be attached to knowing that what you're doing is unique, and that you're making a contribution to society, not simply reinventing the wheel.

If your passion is teaching and serving, you don't have to work in an inner-city school or nonprofit organization as your adventureprise. Instead, your adventureprise might look like marketing support for a large German pharmaceutical firm, as in the case of Daranee Russell. Daranee is well paid and finds great satisfaction in marketing HIV drugs that prolong life and help the body fight HIV-related infections. She is an educator whose job involves teaching doctors and community-based HIV support organizations how these pharmaceuticals work. She meets with and encourages patients and also functions as a local clearinghouse for information on available services, key contacts, and new developments.

Marketing and sales can truly be forms of service. For example, if you knew of a place that sold gasoline for a dollar less per gallon than anywhere else, wouldn't you tell your friends about it? Selling a product may not be exactly the same thing, since, often when we benefit directly from selling a product or service, making money corrupts the purity of our intentions. But when you recommend products and services from the level of consciousness of the greater self, you possess a purity of intention when sharing a product or service that you believe does more than simply put cash in your pocket. Selling or marketing at this level of consciousness is a form of service.

The concept of network marketing has been a turnoff for many people primarily because it pushes people beyond their comfort zone and feels invasive. Yet more than 20 million people in the United States are involved in it in one form or another. One of the attractions of working as part of a multilevel marketing company is participation in a community and the opportunity to grow personally. I call it "adventureprise in a box," with the caveat that, while this may be an adventure, network marketing may not always be the enterprise of your soul. But you won't know for sure unless you follow your intuition and see, from the perspective of a broader consciousness, what opportunities exist for you in a specific company. You may find that marketing hygiene products or supplements feels like traditional selling, and that helping people change their lives as part of a community resonates beautifully with your soul. You may get a kick from it.

What typically happens to many sales representatives is that they join companies with the expectation that "the business opportunity" will solve their personal financial needs without them having to change the consciousness that created their problems in the first place. In truth, the most successful independent sales representatives are focused on the greater benefits that their products and their sales opportunities offer. Randy Gage, a leading prosperity coach for the USANA Health Sciences company, and author of *Why You're Dumb, Sick, and Broke*, points out that the products themselves offer benefits, and the business opportunities they create for distributors are a great way for them to work through their issues related to prosperity, deserving, and wholeness while making money. Results often come only after there's been a shift in consciousness.

Principle 4. Be Willing to Play Big

One of the key reasons entrepreneurs (as opposed to adventurepreneurs) fail is that they haven't healed their counterfeit beliefs and so carry too many spiritual liabilities. As noted earlier, people who seek to be entrepreneurs undertake business ventures for a number of reasons, such as to prove themselves (gain approval), to be their own bosses (exercise control), and to create wealth (gain external power). Most entrepreneurs focus only a little on their connection with Spirit, because they don't yet realize that material results spring out of a nonmaterial source. Their path of adventureprise is designed to raise their consciousness.

The world is waiting for you to think big and emerge through your adventureprise as a full-blown adventurepreneur. As bestselling author and spiritual teacher Marianne Williamson so aptly puts it in *A Return to Love*, "Your playing small does not serve the world."[10]

Nor does your playing small allow you to soar from the self-cherishing enterprise of life to adventureprise, the enterprise of the soul. If you choose to stay in the comfort zone of fear, rather than embrace the occasional discomfort of change and empowerment, your life will look, feel, and be a series of "could haves" or "might have beens."

More important, if your life has always been about chasing dollars or taking on two jobs in order to make ends meet, the greatest gift you can give yourself is the permission to break out of that cycle by developing talents and interests that truly call you to action. Seek to understand your unique spiritual assets. Open to receive a flow of support. Then the business of adventureprise will take care of the adventureprise in your business.

Few individual things you do will ever change the world. But many things you do will change your own world. Since you are an important piece of the fabric of life, your adventureprise and your world are important to both the present and the future of spiritual consciousness. As you move into the harmony of adventureprise, you may trust that you will empower and inspire others to do the same.

EXERCISES FOR YOUR SOUL

The following three exercises will assist you in developing your adventureprise.

MANAGING YOUR SPIRITUAL PORTFOLIO

Make a Daily "To-Be" List

In the morning, before you begin your day, jot down a simple to-do list for the day ahead, leaving blank spaces between the various items where you can make notes. Next, reflect upon the spiritual assets you would like to call on in the pursuit of each action. For example, in writing this chapter I called on creativity, persistence, ability with language, and intuition. List the assets you believe would enable you to feel connection, joy, and ease while you're doing everything you do. In essence, you are creating a "to-be" list for the day.

At the end of the day, review what took place during the day. Did your day flow, or did you encounter challenges? Were there any connections (other than you) between the different events? Were you able to achieve the state of beingness you envisioned in the morning? Did preparing yourself to call upon your spiritual assets make it easier to activate them?

PERSONAL EXPERIENCE

Choose Passion and Fun

Select an activity in your life that's fun and that you feel passionate about. For the time being, let this be something other than the activity you're currently employed in. If you love hanging out in the park with your dog, you could choose that. If you enjoy tango dancing, choose that. Now, imagine two ways that this enthusiasm could become a business and serve as the enterprise of your soul. Write down exactly what type of product or service you would provide, how you would be paid, and who would benefit.

MEDITATION

Unify the Enterprise of the Soul

Sit quietly in a comfortable position. Close your eyes and breathe easily. As you enter a calm, meditative state, imagine yourself being surrounded by a yellow light that symbolizes the events of your everyday life. Notice how this energy feels. Does it have a harmonious feel, or does it have waves? Does it have dark spots or feel uncomfortable in places?

Now imagine a white light emanating from your solar plexus that represents harmony, joy, love, and fulfillment. Notice how this energy feels to you. Does the light outside you feel a bit disconnected from the light of your soul? Imagine the light of your soul expanding and growing larger until it not only envelops the yellow light but also expands as far as you're willing to let it. How far are you willing to let the light of your soul expand?

Observe the sensations in your body. Notice whether the yellow light has turned white. Do you feel more unity in the energy of your soul? Can you sense the essence of this energy? How would you describe it? Hold this energy for two minutes so you can savor it. Then, finish the meditation by taking the energy into your heart and allowing it to fill every part of you.

6

YOUR STAKEHOLDERS

The Power of Connection

We cannot live for ourselves alone. Our lives are connected by a thousand invisible threads, and along these sympathetic fibers, our actions run as causes and return to us as results.

— HENRY MELVILL, "Partaking in Other Men's Sins"

You have seen that, when spiritual capital is invested with loving intentionality, it flows into fresh opportunities, abundant creativity and resources, and deep and lasting fulfillment for the soul. In adventureprise, success is love magnified by the power of collective intention and participation. So it's especially important to encourage the circulation of love through your social networks. You have the support of an enormous number of stakeholders — far more than you will ever know — in ever-widening circles, who share a vested interest in your success and well-being. Getting these people involved in your adventureprise and contributing their spiritual assets to yours is the fifth step in the soul currency program.

In the material world (the realm where business imitates life) the direct connection between a corporation and its various stakeholders is obvious. Shareholders have a stake in the successful running of a business (they receive dividends), as do its managers and employees (they receive wages and opportunities), its suppliers (they receive payment), its customers (they receive goods and services), and the broader community (it receives taxes, residents, street activity, social stability, and more). It can be argued that even industry competitors benefit from the activities of a healthy business, because companies in thriving industries adopt the best practices of their field and recruit skilled talent from within the ranks of competing firms.

When we think of the stakeholders in our own lives, it's easy to forget how many people truly are served by our success and happiness. We tend to think of the people who are immediately connected to us, such as our mates, children, parents, siblings, friends, and business partners, as benefiting from our presence in their lives. Yet this list barely scratches the surface of our network of stakeholders, which in fact encompasses humanity and all life on Earth.

Furthermore, we typically discount the importance of our spiritual capital to the wider world. Most of us seldom consider that our simple presence could be a form of grace for another being because we intangibly give and receive energy. From the level of self-cherishing consciousness, we are materialistic and look only at what is owed: "He owes me big time!" "You owe me a dinner." "She'd be nothing without my help." From the consciousness of connection, it's easy to recognize that we give, and that the flow of giving then moves forward — even if we give to those who don't give back to us directly.

People thousands of miles apart can positively and negatively affect each other's energy fields. Scientists like biologist Rupert Sheldrake and Marilyn Schlitz, the director of research for the Institute of Noetic Sciences, have documented the power of collective energy in influencing outcomes. In his book *Prayer Is Good*

Medicine, Dr. Larry Dossey writes about the notable effects that group prayer can produce on healing. By moving out of a self-cherishment mode of being, you can learn to tap into the energy of your global stakeholders, those uncounted numbers of people who consciously and unconsciously send you love, goodwill, and the energy of success in each moment. Also, by counting yourself as a stakeholder in the lives of millions of people on this planet, you recognize your place in a field of ever-expanding consciousness.

STAKEHOLDERS IN YOUR LIFE

I love the 2007 Verizon television ad that pans to an unassuming young man who resembles Woody Allen, and then pans over to a suave-looking gangster and his two henchmen. "Did you come alone?" the gangster asks, as if a big deal is about to go down. "Yes," says the Woody Allen look-alike as he takes out his cell phone. "Then who are they?" asks the gangster, gesturing off-camera. In back of the young man are hundreds of people, maybe thousands, who represent the human network that makes his cell phone work.

Stakeholders in your life are linked to you through powerful, often invisible connections. Direct connections can be drawn to members of your family, friends, and business associates, but other connections exist among members of the communities you participate in. Your network reaches out through and beyond your acquaintances to people you don't know.

Being vested in another person's financial success seemingly takes place outside us on the material level. However, this draws on a limited definition of the word *being*. We can feel vested in another person's well-being. This takes place inside us on an energetic level.

When you abide in the consciousness of the greater you, your good is the good of the entire world. A farmer in Iowa who sends surplus crops to the organization Feed the Children is honoring his global connections. So is a five-year-old child living in upstate New York who contributes her weekly allowance to an agency serving famine-stricken Darfur. I have heard the Dalai Lama call people such as these "stakeholders in humanity." The recipients of crops and funds won't know where they come from specifically, yet these gifts are gratefully accepted. Most of us never meet all our stakeholders, any more than Bill Gates, the president of Microsoft, gets to know all of his company's stakeholders, or the president of the United States knows each person who voted in the last election.

The stakeholders in your life are a sweeping and broad-ranging group of individuals. Your education, for example, was paid for by a vast number of anonymous taxpaying citizens and assisted by the efforts of your parents and teachers, who, as a result, have a residual interest in your personal development and accomplishments. According to ESR Economic Research, the average direct investment in labor, expenses, and education made per pupil per year from kindergarten through high school is about $8,745 a year.[1] The indirect costs may be at least that, if not more.

The actual annual expenses of higher education are at least double that amount. They also may be partially subsidized, or perhaps entirely paid for, by your various stakeholders. Through my contributions to my alma mater, Amherst College, I know that state- and privately owned colleges cover approximately 60 percent of their direct costs through tuition and the rest through contributed capital from your indirect stakeholders, people responsible for paying taxes and purchasing education bonds, and people who make donations to these institutions. If you qualify for a student loan, the funds are advanced to you from both public and private stakeholders and people who own stock in the financial institutions. Thousands more people have directly or indirectly participated in every experience in your life.

Almost everything you do involves stakeholders. For example, if you choose to go to church, your donation (if it's like the average person's) generally is not sufficient to cover the costs of your portion of the church's operation. As assistant pastor of a church in South Florida, I have checked these figures and know that to turn on the lights and run the service every week costs the church about thirty-five dollars per member. So if you put ten dollars in the collection box, the church has to cover the remaining twenty-five dollars. Other donors and *their* network of stakeholders have partially paid for your privilege to attend. The U.S. tax code exempts churches and nonprofits from paying taxes, which is a form of subsidy paid to churchgoers by nearly all of us. If you drive to a nearby restaurant to go dancing, you utilize public roads, buy gasoline, and pay taxes and tolls. The restaurant pays business taxes, and any building it leases space from probably pays property taxes, and so on. Because you're a member of a community, your resources are interlinked with your neighbors' resources.

The huge number of anonymous people who have stakes in our lives is too mind-boggling for most of us to translate from an intellectual concept into reality. We often require stakeholders to take a supportive action for us overtly before we allow ourselves to bring them into our hearts. At times we think we're alone, but this is an illusion. The best thing about acknowledging that millions have served us is that, when we do acknowledge it, it becomes clear that in the ordinary course of living we also have directly and indirectly affected millions of other people.

YOUR STAKE IN THE LIVES OF OTHERS

Just as you have stakeholders, you are a direct stakeholder in the lives of an enormous number of people. By my estimation, you've already touched millions. Your investment in those around you might be as simple as a smile or a kind word of encouragement that gives someone else permission to be loving, or it may take the form of raising funds to feed a million hungry people in a drought-stricken country. There are many ways your soul currency ripples beyond your direct presence, like the ripples formed when a stone is dropped into a quiet pond. Most people tend to forget the good things they do for others.

If you believe that only doing great things affects other people's lives, consider Mother Teresa's admonishment to do small things with great love. Every small thing done with kindness and love increases the flow of soul currency in the world. This includes opening doors for strangers, letting someone in a hurry go ahead of you in the checkout line, and having friendly chats with the postal carrier. All things people do affect other people. We often feel good when others overcome their challenges, or take satisfaction and empathize with them when they experience deep love.

One of the tennis players I most enjoyed watching compete during the past two decades was Andre Agassi, who so perfectly understood the power of his stakeholders, a fan base that grew as he rose to become one of the greatest players in the history of the game. Agassi is one of only five male players to have won all four Grand Slam singles events (the Australian Open, the French Open, Wimbledon, and the U.S. Open) during his career. He is the *only* player in the Open Era (after 1968) to have won every Grand Slam men's singles title, the Tennis Masters Cup, and an Olympic gold medal and been part of a winning Davis Cup team.[2] He won seventeen Association of Tennis Professionals Masters Series tournaments — more than any other player. Now in retirement, he's earned more admiration for his charitable work.

As a young player coming up, Agassi was rebellious. He wore his hair long, sported an earring, and often played tempestuously on the court. But he always appreciated his gallery of fans. Once Agassi began to appreciate his natural gifts of keen eyesight and exceptional hand-eye coordination, his matches became a form of artistry. He could stand inside the baseline and return 125-mile-per-hour serves with equal speed. His ground strokes were so fluid and perfectly timed that he could force his opponents to run from corner to corner or watch his shots whip by them when they came to the net. He wore his opponents down, yet he was gracious in both victory and defeat. He celebrated his victories by acknowledging the fans with two-handed kisses blown in all four directions of the arena.

Agassi transformed the goodwill of the people who enjoyed his tennis career into an abundant flow of spiritual capital. The Andre Agassi Charitable Foundation serves more than two thousand children a year through its funding of a Boys and Girls Club, which runs programs to promote athletic potential. In 2001, he started and funded the Andre Agassi College Preparatory Academy to help at-risk youth go to college and get a degree. Ironically, Agassi had cut short his own formal education at age sixteen because he was so eager to turn pro.

Agassi's remarks after he had played his final professional tennis match in Arthur Ashe Stadium at the 2006 U.S. Open in Flushing, New York, eloquently express his understanding of interconnection and the power of personal stakeholders in all of life. He addressed the crowd from the court: "Thanks. The scoreboard said I lost today, but what the scoreboard doesn't say is what it is I have found. And over the last twenty-one years, I have found loyalty. You have pulled for me on the court and also in life. I've found inspiration. You have willed me to succeed sometimes even in my lowest moments. And I've found generosity. You have given me your shoulders to stand on to reach for my dreams, dreams I could have never reached without you. Over the last twenty-one years, I have found you. And I will take you and the memory of you with me for the rest of my life. Thank you."[3]

The network that supports you, and that you support, is the human representation of your soul currency. Multiply this by the ever-widening circle of people you are at the center of, and you can understand how the power of one person easily expands into the power of many. Most people tap only a fraction of the power available to them. This unused power is much like an unused software feature (for example, a photo editor or a financial spreadsheet) on a computer they've had so long that they're surprised when they find this feature for the first time. In your adventureprise, if you can embrace your connections, it will unleash the power of your greatest potential.

HOW CONNECTION SERVES ADVENTUREPRISE

To be aware of connection is to be grateful for how interdependent we are. To be unaware is to be unconscious of the gifts and contributions constantly being exchanged. It is to miss the beauty of Spirit. In a world of energy, money is only part of the equation. We may earn a salary, but it would all be for naught without the willingness of the farmer, fisherman, auto repairman, and countless others who play roles in bringing, for example, bread to our dinner table. Awareness of connection is the catalyst for broadening our perspective.

Think about the infinite network of connection we live in, a network that is constantly in motion, alive, and vibrantly creative, catalyzed by the invisible hand of Spirit. The key to leading a fulfilled and prosperous life is to recognize our connection to the intelligence of source energy. The greater our sense of connection, the more love we can share, the more love we can receive, and the greater the sense of wholeness we feel within. Here's why. If one man or woman gives another an apple and in exchange receives a different apple, that person still has only one apple. But when one man or woman gives another an idea, and the other in exchange gives the first his or her own idea, they both end up having more than two ideas, because ideas stimulate more ideas!

There are two ways to get people to contribute their spiritual assets to your adventureprise. One is to draw the "right" people to you through intentionality and then ask for their contribution directly. Another is to share your vision with visionaries, describe the greater benefits to those who are drawn by the importance of return, and talk about safety, and the right thing to do, for those who are still operating in a mode of self-cherishing consciousness. Your already-existing stakeholders, who may or may not be conscious of their roles, are the ones who participate in your ventures, help you when you're seeking to find a job, and get involved in your social networking. Anything you need can be found through your circle of connections.

Groups focused on a single goal prosper through their experience of collaboration and cooperation. Collective intentionality brings coherence — the synergistic rhythm of a single organism — to our actions. It enables us to tap into source energy and, therefore, produces greater love, abundance, and deeper fulfillment for the entire group and for all those whom the group is in contact with. Collaboration and cooperation are material-world representations of unity.

The power of collective consciousness transcends corporate boundaries and human-made obstacles. Don Tapscott and

Anthony Williams, authors of *Wikinomics*, begin their book with a story of Goldcorp, a publicly held Canadian gold mining company concerned that its gold reserves would be depleted. The company was faced with the expensive and uncertain proposition of investing large amounts in exploration. But the chief executive officer was considering another approach, offering a program of collaboration and tapping into the expertise and experience of others, including possible competitors. The only problem was that he would have to open up access to much of the data on all their properties, the sort of data that every gold mining company guarded jealously.

The chief executive did the unthinkable: he posted all the data on the Internet, along with the offer that, if anyone came up with a well-documented proposition showing where to drill on their properties, the company would share the revenues if they were successful. Instead of getting a lot of crank propositions, the company found that nearly 80 percent of the many responses they received from many sources eventually led to commercial discoveries. The company, instead of having declining reserves, identified potential reserves that it estimated would produce more than thirty times what it annually produced.

By seeing the power of connecting and cocreating with stakeholders, the old paradigm of win-lose has given way to collaboration and cooperation in many industries. For example, the communications and computer industry has benefited from doing collaborative research to set industry protocols for data, voice, and video transmission. Chip makers are collaborating on new technologies that use light as a connector in order to make chips smaller and faster. The television and display industry has been able to introduce vastly improved products at lower costs through collaboration. Doing the unthinkable, such as sharing development costs with one's traditionally bitter industry rivals, has had the effect of expanding the market faster for everyone involved.

Collective intention is unstoppable. Sometimes it draws out of us a tremendous commitment of resources and leads to a major physical effort, such as building China's Three Gorges Dam. Spanning the Yangtze River, this dam, the world's largest hydroelectric project, will become fully operational in 2011. For more than a thousand years, the powerful Yangtze River has overflowed its banks during the rainy season, sweeping away villages and precious topsoil, ruining crops, and drowning hundreds of farmers and their families. The flooding has affected more than a million acres of land and has often caused massive starvation. Designed to both generate electricity and control massive spring flooding, the dam has cost more than $200 billion to build, required enormous engineering acumen, and involved moving 1.4 million people, those displaced by the rising waters. It takes a clear, unwavering vision to see a project through on this scale.

Another event harnessing the power of the collective imagination illustrates how intention precedes action. The year 1985 saw the first New Year's World Peace Meditation, a concept and event conceived of by John Randolph Price, which I participated in at the Cathedral Church of Saint John the Divine in New York City. It was designed to coordinate people worldwide to sustain a unified intention. Three years later, on December 31, 1988, as I recall, organizers of the fourth annual event estimated participation in excess of a hundred thousand people meditating for harmony, peace, and freedom on the planet. That might seem like a rather small number of participants; however, according to research conducted under the direction of Maharishi Mahesh Yogi at his university, the square root of 1 percent of the population in any one area can create a field of energy powerful enough to affect the entire population.[4] In 1988, there were approximately 5.2 billion people on earth, and the square root of 1 percent, or 52 million that year, was approximately 7,211 people.

Was it an accident that less than twelve months after the World Peace Meditation, the energy surrounding the planet supported the disassembly of the Berlin Wall, the reunification of East and West Germany, and fall of communist totalitarian governments in Czechoslovakia, Poland, Hungary, Bulgaria, and parts of the former Soviet Union? Political scientists and activists were stunned at the rapidity of the departure of firmly entrenched governments in response to an alteration in consciousness. If the U.S. government had attempted a military solution to accomplish the same thing, similar to what the United States has attempted by pursuing the Iraq War, we might still be fighting a world war begun to resolve the cold war, possibly millions of lives would have been lost, and we would be no closer now to achieving freedom and democracy than we were when we started.

Being conscious of the oneness of all things — and of the individual roles we play as members of the whole — enables us to strengthen our social networks while affirming our participation in the flow of love. Connection opens the heart to the greater self. It helps us transcend our self-cherishing consciousness and move in the direction of service to the greater good. When we perceive life as unity, life in turn supports us — and sometimes in the most unexpected ways.

WORLD CONSCIOUSNESS
AND GLOBAL STAKEHOLDERS

Reverend David Owen Ritz, in his Keys to the Kingdom prosperity course, is fond of saying, "The world was not given to you; you were given to the world."[5] You must go beyond your immediate circle of stakeholders to allow yourself a grander view of both your stakeholders and those whose lives you have a stake in. Your perspective on wars, famine, and disasters may change when you realize that, whether you like it or not, you have a responsibility to take action *first* by transforming your own consciousness (which may or may not lead to taking further action) and *then* by seeing it reflected in the elevation of collective consciousness.

When you tap into the global consciousness that connects us, you tap into the most authentic, unlimited source of spiritual capital there is. This creative source builds countries, has lifted millions of people from poverty into prosperity, and is a catalyst that will enable you to recognize the Oneness of all life. All it takes is for one person — you — to wake up to the need in front of you.

In 1996, young Benjamin Quinto participated in a small discussion and networking session of international nongovernmental organizations at the United Nations in New York City. He was inspired to meet a roomful of people whose lives were dedicated to global problem solving. At the same time, however, he was shocked to learn that few young people were involved. After reading the UN Charter and observing its call for the participation of young people, he set out to create a United Nations Youth Assembly. After three years of consultation with UN bureaucrats, international organizations, and youth from all over the world, he concluded that the UN could not create a youth assembly without youth representation.

Many youth organizations around the world were getting involved in global governance but needed better organization. In July 1999, the United Youth Conference convened with twenty young people from twelve different countries. Together they founded the Global Youth Action Network to create a clearinghouse for today's youth movements; to encourage collaboration, understanding, and tolerance; and to promote youth activism around the world. Today, the Global Youth Action Network is one of the largest networks of youth organizations ever created. It acts as an incubator of global partnerships and as a global information provider. It's known for its role in increasing youth participation in the United Nations and for coorganizing Global Youth Service Day with Youth Service America, the world's largest annual celebration of young volunteers. Millions of youth participate each April in more than a hundred countries. The leader of the group at the time of this writing is a young German woman named Franziska Seel.[6]

That Muhammad Yunus received the Nobel Peace Prize for his pioneering work in economically lifting the poor in Sri Lanka through microlending reminds us that, when we are active stakeholders and invest our spiritual capital, we open up the flow of soul currency. Microlending involves very small amounts of money, for which the investor receives interest when the loan is repaid. In the physical world, microlending is a grassroots movement in which those who have resources invest them in local entrepreneurs in developing countries, who use those resources to change their lives. But in the multisensory energy world of the greater you, investment vehicles such as microlending and grassroots microfinance organizations are reflections of how we invest our spiritual assets — how we microlend our spiritual capital in the form of encouragement, connections, and action to those around us.

Kiva, founded in 2005, a highly successful prototype of peer-to-peer microlending, is one of the few organizations that enable the lender to actually experience having a stake in the success of the borrower. This organization believes that having a relationship with the people to whom we lend brings love and satisfaction fully into our hearts. Success stories open our hearts, take us out of the self-cherishment mode, and put us in the full flow of our soul currency. Kiva's website enables individuals to go on the

Internet and, with the click of a computer key, lend small amounts of money to selected poor entrepreneurs in developing countries around the world.

According to Kiva's website, "Kiva began modestly in March 2005 in Uganda when seven businesses requesting a total of $3,500 in loans were posted on Kiva.org as a trial run of the new microfinancing service organization. These poor entrepreneurs included a goat herder, a fishmonger, a cattle farmer, and a restaurateur. Six months later every loan had been repaid."[7] Since its inception, Kiva has grown from a small personal project to one of the world's largest microfinance facilitators, connecting entrepreneurs with millions of dollars in loans from tens of thousands of small lenders around the world who enjoy making money while doing good.

Matt and Jessica Flannery, the husband-and-wife team who founded Kiva, already had a consciousness that went beyond them. At the time they started Kiva, their most significant realization was that they would attract more funds for the impoverished people around the world if donors had the opportunity to know more about the people receiving funds. Having a direct stake in someone's life is a compelling way to go beyond your self-cherishing consciousness and into consciousness of the greater you. In dedicating their lives to the adventureprise of Kiva, and giving up other potentially good conventional job opportunities, Matt and Jessica opened themselves to a greater seva consciousness that made them stakeholders in humanity, not simply stakeholders in the individuals whose lives they helped.

On an inner level, we share our spiritual capital in much the same way. You don't have to go overseas to an economically deprived area to invest your spiritual capital. As a stakeholder in the lives of countless people, you are doing this each day more times than you can count. I've found that the greatest way I can "microlend" a hand to those who are struggling is to help them see their own magnificence. I do this by reminding them of their oneness with Spirit and encouraging them with the thought that, whatever Spirit can do, it must do it through them. Through timely encouragement and inspiration, we invest our spiritual capital in the world. We strengthen and build our social networks exponentially, meaning that one person connects to ten or twelve others, who each connect to four or fifteen more, who each connect to ten more — suddenly you're reaching millions. And by our very action, the people we share our spiritual capital with become an important part of our stakeholders network.

By participating in the greater good, you give yourself permission to more deeply experience love and connection, and you give others around you permission to do the same. As Rabindranath Tagore, a Bengali poet and winner of the Nobel Prize for Literature has written, "I slept and dreamt that life was joy. I awoke and saw that life was service. I acted and behold, service was joy."[8]

CREATING ACTIVE STAKEHOLDERS

Author, speaker, and social entrepreneur Mark Victor Hansen is fond of saying, "My network is my net worth." No one knows this better than he does, as a result of cocreating the bestselling *Chicken Soup for the Soul* series of books, which have connected him with more than 250 million readers in a hundred different countries and made him a multimillionaire. Networks are like fields in which we can grow the crops of greater success. By planting seeds of intention in these fields, we can cultivate the power of collective consciousness, which is like fertilizing and nourishing our spiritual capital. Hansen has wisely parlayed his book series' name recognition into a group of thriving enterprises, including a recently established charitable foundation that supports youth empowerment, literacy, and the eradication of hunger and poverty. Because of his financial success, he is now empowered to serve humanity on a wider scale and has consciously accepted a tremendous role as a stakeholder in the lives of others.

By promoting stakeholder activism, the organization Ashoka takes the concept of stakeholdership one step further. According to the organization's website, "Ashoka is a global association of the leading social entrepreneurs, men and women determined to come up with system-changing solutions for the world's most urgent problems. Since 1981, over 1,800 leading entrepreneurs have been elected as Ashoka Fellows, for which they are granted living stipends, professional support, and access to a network of peers in more than 60 countries. . . . Our Fellows inspire others to adopt and spread innovations, demonstrating to people everywhere that we all have the potential to be powerful changemakers."[9]

Bill Drayton, chief executive officer and founder of Ashoka, was a highly successful entrepreneur by the time he finished college. A former McKinsey and Company executive and advisor to President Clinton, Drayton coined the word *changemaker* to show how every person affects others. Ashoka, which in Sanskrit means "without sorrow," was named after an enlightened Indian king who had learned from sad experience that peace was more powerful than war. As an organization, Ashoka has taken the concept of changemaker to new levels.

In a speech at the 2007 Clinton Global Initiative Conference, Drayton cited a local example of the difference a single changemaker can make. A young African American boy was brought to Ashoka's attention by the Cambridge, Massachusetts, police, who felt that, although he had been in and out of trouble, he had some special entrepreneurial talents. This led to the creation of an organization where the young man taught neighborhood boys and girls how to build and rebuild bicycles. The police had a huge stock of unclaimed bicycles, so each person taking the thirty-five-hour class graduated with a free bicycle.

The 2nd Gear Bike Shop today not only sells bikes, it also enables kids who can't afford a bike to earn one with ten hours of service and fifteen hours of classes. The program, which teaches self-esteem and other life skills, has been expanded to teach computer classes as well. The young man who started it all, and who once nearly ended up jail, went on to college.[10]

Online social networking is often just as effective as face-to-face networking. The Internet has helped us to appreciate the power of connection more than anything else in our society. There has been an explosion of social, professional, and affinity websites whose premise is connection and shared interest. Again, as we network, we are reminded both of the magnificence and the foibles of our humanity, as well as the spirit moving through us with love.

Yahoo groups have enabled the formation of small online communities, and there are numerous other avenues by which others have come together. Wikipedia estimates that, as of January 2008, more than two hundred social networking sites exist, with an estimated 400–600 million individual members total.

The power of the network arises when intention meets connection. It's then that you realize that learning to keep track of your network is much like setting up a savings account to enable your spiritual capital to become social capital. Websites such as Facebook.com put us in touch with greater and greater numbers of people. They enable us to share our humanness — the things that give us our joy, our fears, and our uniqueness. Although many of the social networking sites on the Internet began as opportunities to get to know people, businesses have begun to use these extensively to market products and services. An investment banker specializing in private equity investments benefits regularly from his connection to the nearly four thousand contacts he has in his LinkedIn.com account.

If you've never experienced an online social network before, begin by joining one for free and creating a profile so you can explore that network's activities. Some require an invitation to join; others are open to anyone who visits the website's home page. None are especially hard to access. An online social network is just one possible system for staying in touch with a relatively wide community and expanding your connection to diverse resources.

Recruiters will tell you that most jobs are typically found through "soft network" connections (for example, someone who knows someone else whose brother may have an opportunity for the job-seeker). Our soft networks, those where we seem to be only tenuously connected, extend so far outward from us that we may not even realize their full potential. But they are so important that even recruiters themselves invest much of their time establishing networks of referrals in their daily calls to prospects and through the Internet and other opportunities.

Most recently both my sons changed their jobs. My younger son, Jonathan Chu, who was unhappy in his position as an investment analyst for a hedge-fund group, set an intention to find another job in the same field where he would be happier and well paid. He networked until he heard of an opportunity at a larger money-management firm from a friend who worked there. My eldest son, Chris, the video game programmer, also felt he needed a change. By setting an intention, he set in motion the energy of creative transformation. For a while he had been corresponding online with friends in Singapore and had even taken a vacation there. He became open to the possibility of moving to the island nation for the right deal. Within weeks he was contacted via a recruiter in his LinkedIn.com network, and through this contact he began discussions with an American company that had relocated its video-game development operations to Singapore. He received an excellent offer and within one month moved to Singapore.

Networks are the gateway to greater consciousness as well as to jobs. The Gaia Community (formerly known as Zaadz) is one of the largest consciousness-raising websites, with more than seventy-five thousand members. Its website encompasses a diverse array of communities of interest, such as conscious capitalism, spirituality in the workplace, eco-lifestyles, alternative health and healing, and religion and spirituality.[11] This is an example of how social networking helps us stretch. The site enables users, who may have never before taken pictures with a digital camera, to put together first-time videos about themselves and what makes them feel passionate. Other active conscious networks include ConsciousLivingPartnership.org, Ted.com, SharedVision.com, and ThinkHolistic.com. Any like-minded community offers safety to individuals who would feel uneasy about introducing themselves at a networking event. Many otherwise shy people are willing to post their innermost thoughts where hundreds of thousands of people can read them.

Professional websites are another part of the fabric of peer-to-peer networking. The Management, Spirituality, and Religion division of the Academy of Management is the largest association of business school academicians, researchers, practitioners, and doctoral students. It has enabled frank discussion of research methodology and served as a conduit for partnering and communication, for finding resources of all types, and for publicizing and discussing areas of interest. Another example drawn from my own experience is the Association of Fundraising Professionals, an organization of which I am a member. When I was exploring the value of buying a certain type of software, I placed a phone call to the president of the Fort Lauderdale chapter. He agreed to send out an email to chapter members asking anyone with feedback on that software package to reply. Within forty-five minutes, I had spoken to the executive directors of three nonprofit organizations of different sizes and was quickly able to make a decision.[12]

Your email inbox (yes, the one in which you often get Internet spam) will be a gateway for many of your greatest and most unexpected stakeholders. Perhaps you've never thought of someone who sends you inspirational mail as a stakeholder — perhaps you perceive this person as more of a nuisance. But if you find yourself resenting someone who is sending you thoughtful and potentially inspiring messages, you might want to check your receiving issues. One particular email I received last year contained a link to a flash movie titled *The Interview with God*. Essentially a poem with images, it has been so inspirational and moving to its viewers that it's been shared more than 6 million times and has become a source of revenue for a foundation.

Another email brought to my attention *Pray Always*, a poignant series of pictures of people of diverse faiths in prayer compiled by web designer Lisa Cameron, owner of Whispering Stars Web Design. *Pray Always* is set to the heart-opening music of singer-songwriter Daniel Nahmod ("When I Pray"). I find this four-minute video such a powerful way to connect with the spirit of humanity that I watch it several times a week in order to center myself, become more present, and heighten my awareness of my natural, deep connectedness with others before doing work or interacting.[13]

CREATE FROM A GREATER CONSCIOUSNESS

When you create anything from a state of connected consciousness, you are not simply creating by means of what your ego recognizes as yourself. Rather you are also creating with the energy of all your collective stakeholders. The power of connection embodied by even the most ethereal network of relationships has immense creative potential. Even if your soul's adventureprise takes the form of a profit-making business, it may serve a vision that positively affects the lives of thousands of people. An enterprise launched by an artist in Canada did this in a most unlikely way. I was able to piece together this remarkable story from many interviews with the artist and most of the participants, and from visits to the neighborhood in Canada where it took place. I have taken some artistic liberties myself where the details aren't known.

Albert Younan had just finished his breakfast at a Tim Horton's Restaurant near his home in a suburb of Toronto. Stepping out into the slightly overcast day, he noticed that the brisk air and budding trees exuded the energy of spring. He decided that today he would walk rather than drive to spend a few hours with his cousin Sammy, whose auto repair shop was around the corner. As he cut through the rear parking lot of the restaurant, he saw an unkempt man dressed in dirty clothes digging through the restaurant's dumpster. His curiosity piqued, Albert thought he would offer him the uneaten breakfast muffin he had stuck in his pocket.

The unkempt man was apparently so intent on scrounging for food and what seemed like waste cardboard and paper that he didn't see Albert approach. Albert was shocked that he recognized him. He was a local artist named Shwan Ziwar, who Albert would occasionally see at his cousin's garage, as they were friends. He hadn't seen much of Shwan lately. All three of them had at one time been refugees from Iraq. Albert had come over more than two decades earlier, had gone into real estate and bought and fixed up properties, and then had become a mortgage broker. Sammy was a thriving auto mechanic who worked magic on neighborhood cars. Shwan had lived in many places in Europe before coming to Canada.

Shwan purported to be an artist, which, in Albert's mind and in the minds of most of the neighbors, meant that he didn't have a job. "Everybody wants to be an artist or an actor," he thought. At least he could help out a fellow human being in a time of need. When Albert reached the dumpster, there was an uncomfortable silence. Shwan explained that he was looking for materials to paint on. "And food too?" asked Albert, who noticed that Shwan had taken out and put aside some uneaten bagels and packets of jam. "And food too," said Shwan softly.

What followed was the first of many meals at the Younan's home. Then Shwan, who lived in the basement of a nearby Kia auto dealership with only a toilet and sink, took a shower and washed his clothes. He was deeply grateful to Albert and his family. He explained that he had sold many of his paintings, but that some art dealers owed him thousands of dollars and had never paid him. He was several months behind in his rent. He didn't have money to buy needed medicine. And now he had no money for food.

Yet he insisted that he would continue to paint. He told a still skeptical Albert that he'd created many paintings that now hung in museums in Europe and galleries in the United States, and that his work had been collected by an ever-expanding group of Asian collectors from Taiwan and other Asian countries. "Come to my gallery," Shwan urged his new benefactor. There was something in his voice that overcame Albert's natural skepticism. Intrigued, Albert went to the gallery.

The entrance to Shwan's gallery was a long, steep stairway that disappeared into the darkness of a basement as large as a medium-size high school gymnasium. It reeked of garbage. A single path wound among piles and piles of paintings, building materials, and a sea of discarded paint cans, brushes, garbage bags, and similar art supplies. In places, the piles rose to waist height and cast fantastic shadows on the walls. The ambience was a mixture of squalor and splendor, neglect and genius. Albert found himself gasping as he followed Shwan around the room. The amazing impressionistic paintings that were scattered everywhere took his breath away. Albert, who had set aside his own passion for art to pursue something "more practical," wondered if he had been suddenly transported to a treasure trove out of the *Arabian Nights*. This was a gift that had to be shared with the world.

Albert realized that helping Shwan was going to be a far bigger project than he could undertake alone. His first call was to a business associate named David McClure, chief executive officer of a $200-million real estate development company in western Canada. McClure, who appreciated art, was also mesmerized when he visited Shwan's gallery. He recruited Rick Burley and Steve Chapman to put together a distributorship that would enable Shwan to market his original paintings and sell reproductions through their extensive investor network. Shwan and his new supporters agreed that a portion of every sale would go toward funding a project providing low-cost temporary housing for homeless people, run by the Mustard Seed in Calgary and Edmonton. They truly wanted to do good, and knew that, not only would this help Shwan, but also his art could be used to help numerous other people in difficult circumstances. They also envisioned an arts and music program (still in the planning stages) that would restore dignity to those who were looking to rebuild their lives. Since that day their development project has attracted additional private and public support.

When I arrived at Shwan Ziwar's studio and gallery in Toronto, more than two huge truckloads of garbage and clutter had been removed from the basement of the Kia dealership. New lighting fixtures shone on freshly painted pieces, and some of Shwan's most eye-opening paintings decorated the walls. Shwan is now being helped by several local businesspeople in addition to Albert, each contributing his or her own skills and financial support. His work, which for a few years appeared under the signature "Shwan Dilorenzo," is carried in leading art catalogs and, according to his current distributors, is found globally — in an Italian art museum, palaces in Taiwan, and selected galleries in Europe and the United States. His experience of having to eat out of dumpsters spurred him to envision and lay the groundwork for a program that works with local schools to provide free breakfasts for children whose families encounter financial hardships of their own. When you invest your spiritual capital in adventureprises strengthened by the combined power of your social connections, which serve the good of humanity, you become, in the words of psychologist and author Dr. Jean Houston, a "social artist." Houston envisions social artistry as the "art of enhancing human capacities in the light of social complexity."[14] Her system seeks to bring new ways of thinking, being, and doing to social challenges in the world. Drawing upon its success in training leaders in many organizations throughout the world, social artistry brings state-of-the-art discoveries in human-capacity-building to social transformation. Social artists are leaders in many fields who bring to the canvas of our social reality the same order of passion and skill that an artist brings to his or her art form.

Through social artistry — a higher personality trait that is a spiritual asset — you can access your inner capacity to align yourself with humanity. Ultimately, developing your soul currency will enable you to cocreate the human and social changes needed to make a better world.

EXERCISES FOR YOUR SOUL

The following three exercises will help you explore the power of connection.

MANAGING YOUR SPIRITUAL PORTFOLIO

Recognize Your Life Stakeholders

You'll need paper and a pen for this exercise. Imagine that today is your birthday and you're going to reminisce. Take your age and round it up to the nearest decade. For example, age fifty-four rounds up to sixty. This is your target number. Then make a list of the most important people — living or deceased — in your life. Your list should have the same number of names as your target number (in our example, sixty). Do names come easily to you? If it's difficult to think of enough people, create categories, such as family, friends, teachers, business associates, and so on, to stimulate your recall. Once you've drafted your full list, note how each person has contributed to your well-being. Were you open to receiving it? Reflect on your gratitude. Notice what your physical reactions tell you when you think of each person.

PERSONAL EXPERIENCE

Expand Your Circle of Stakeholders

It is easy to understand the concept of oneness and connection to the world, but it is more difficult to feel it working in your life. What if there were a way to keep track of your network and take it out three generations as it multiplied and spread? With professional networking websites, you can do just that.

For this exercise, you'll need a computer and access to the Internet. Connect to the Internet and go to www.linkedin.com. Begin by going to the sign-in page and opening a LinkedIn account by entering your name, email address, and other details and designating a password. Then go to the profile page and enter information about yourself that you would like others to see. To start with, just put the basic information in, and you can always add to it later.

Now you are ready to start building connections. Adding connections on LinkedIn is by invitation only; you can invite people you know, and those people accept your invitations by confirming that they know you. Once you send invitations, you will be notified when your invitations are accepted. First invite five to ten of your friends and family to join LinkedIn. Then, each day for the first week, send at least five more invitations to business colleagues, acquaintances, and friends. Also, LinkedIn can search the contacts in your email account's address book and let you know which people already have LinkedIn accounts. You may be surprised to discover how many of your contacts are members of LinkedIn, which has more than thirty million members worldwide.

Make each visit to LinkedIn a spiritual experience. Set your intention as you begin, and be mindful of your thoughts and feelings as you uncover the power of present and future stakeholders. Notice your feelings around the names of people who come to mind as you consider whom to invite. Are you excited to invite them, or do you feel uncertain about whether to invite them or whether they might accept? At the end of each visit, before signing off, affirm your thanks and take the experience into your heart.

By the fourth day, you will begin to notice that even with relatively few people in your immediate contact list, LinkedIn will begin to extrapolate the total number of connections you have out to the third generation. Most likely it will be in the hundreds or even thousands. As you add more connections, you will notice that the extrapolated number grows exponentially, with LinkedIn tracking every name. In addition, LinkedIn will tell you as your connections add connections to their contact lists.

Simply put, your LinkedIn account makes a portion of the seemingly invisible network of your millions of stakeholders into a visible, organic network. Go there at least three or four times a week for the first few months, and find opportunities to learn how to use the power of connection.

MEDITATION

Open Up Greater Connection

Sit quietly in a comfortable position. Close your eyes and breathe easily. As soon as you've entered a calm, meditative state, begin to imagine the spiderweb-like energy network of connections stretching in all directions as far as you can see. Each connection appears as a strand of light emanating from your heart. You are at the center of the web, and a vast area around you is lit up with connection and love.

For this meditation, send light to one side of the web, exploring and opening the connections of that web as far as you can go. Then allow yourself to light up as much of the remaining web as your intuition guides you to do. Trust that these connections are already firmly made in consciousness. Notice how you feel when you've expanded your connections with people you might not even know, but in whose lives you are a mutual stakeholder. To complete the meditation, bring your awareness back into your heart and rest for a couple of minutes.

SOUL CURRENCY "MAGIC"

Living in the Flow

I want to know if you can be with joy, mine or your own, if you can dance with wildness and let the ecstasy fill you to the tips of your fingers and toes without cautioning us to be careful, to be realistic, to remember the limitations of being human.

— ORIAH MOUNTAIN DREAMER, *The Invitation*

At the beginning of the book, I told you a story about advice I gave a friend of mine: Our world most definitely needs your greatness, even hungers for it. That's the reason you're reading this book. Our world needs you to wake up and listen to the call of your soul. It needs you to show up and act with purpose, investing your innermost spiritual resources.

Now, as you near the end of the book, you are fully equipped to live in the flow of soul currency. You're aware that the true source of prosperity and fulfillment is love. You've begun to recognize the tremendous inherent value of your spiritual assets and have practiced activating them through focused intentionality. You've begun to imagine and create actual enterprises based on doing what you love in service to the world. You're getting people more involved in your activities. You've developed a process for handling fearful beliefs and are working on paying down your debts to yourself. A clearer vision of your fulfillment is now emerging. In essence, your consciousness has been raised. Therefore it's likely that you are also undergoing a noticeable transformation. You may wonder what this means in the long run and whether it's sustainable.

In our world, it's terribly easy to slip back into the separateness of the human experience and forget the greater truth. And of course, an adventureprise can be run from any level of consciousness. However, self-cherishment presents the greatest challenge to success because of its intense focus on separation and survival. When some of the fears of limitation and loss are healed, adventureprise becomes a collaborative and connecting experience.

At the highest level of consciousness (seva), there is neither attachment to results nor an expectation of return. The greatest benefits in almost every facet of our lives are created at this level. Experiencing a generous flow of love in the form of selfless service involves the returns of greater oneness and aspects of enlightenment. True seva adventureprise is rare, but if you've ever witnessed a soul such as John of God or the Dalai Lama, you'll see they do not lack. The world is constantly thrusting resources upon them so they may continue their service.

The three levels of adventureprise — and for that matter of consciousness — are not mutually exclusive. Rather, frequently the consciousness of self-cherishment overlays the "greater self," and, at even higher levels of adventureprise, seva consciousness overlays connection consciousness. What actually happens is that the ideas of "success" and "return" are redefined as consciousness expands. Upon occasion, most of us experience a kind of recidivism in our focus. We reach a higher level, and then fall back as fear reasserts itself. In general, it takes practice for us to sustain the higher energy state as our perception of return and reward evolves, from measuring "bigness" and financial gain to measuring personal satisfaction and meaning.

Remember, living in the flow of soul currency is not simply an act of faith but also involves a synergy of purpose and intention. Flow is living from a sense of grand sufficiency, but it's not about having. It's about connecting to, and being, the source energy in the universe: love. The greatest rewards come to us when we function as an integral element in Spirit's circulatory system.

WHAT DOES IT MEAN TO LIVE AND WORK IN THE FLOW?

To live fully in soul currency is to remember the essence of who you really are. If you would like to remember, here's some information that will assist you.

- Business opportunities have a purpose higher than making money.
- One source supplies all good, prosperity, and success: Spirit.
- Life must be approached with a loving heart, rather than a knowing head.
- Intuition must balance action.
- Everything that happens is the feedback of a supportive universe.
- An equal exchange of value for value is important.
- There is no separation, not even between you and people or events that present you with obstacles or challenges to overcome.
- There is no need for judgment about the journey each person takes.
- Each person who works alongside you deserves respect and support.

- Prayer creates space for opportunities and the "right" people to enter your life.
- If you open to receive inspiration, Spirit fills in the details.
- The enterprise of your soul is like a present waiting to be unwrapped.

Spirit is present in every aspect of business, especially businesses designed to serve the world in some capacity. Spirit creates the challenges that cause us to stretch, and it helps us heal the counterfeit beliefs that prevent us from making our contributions. Spirit endows our lives with meaning, and it leads us to our creative satisfaction. Enlightened adventurepreneurs bring the greatest resource of all to their business activities: the light of conscious partnership with Spirit. An enlightened adventurepreneur is in a state of being where inner consciousness is constantly creating new choices and new opportunities to help people and improve the condition of the world by building momentum. This inner consciousness is much like the creative, loving intelligence of the universe, which constantly manifests a stream of results for billions of people simultaneously.

You have seen how important it is that consciousness allows you to invest your spiritual capital in more than just personal gain. Learning to invest your spiritual capital is both a habit and a skill that becomes more comfortable as you embrace it and use it in your life. Making use of your soul currency requires you to do less and recognize that you cocreate reality with Spirit, which demonstrates its presence by coming into your life in the form of various people. Here are nine principles for living in the flow.

Principle 1. Help Other People in Order to Help Yourself

My friend Matt Bacak, an Internet marketing guru, is an example of the principle of being rewarded and, in the process, helping others. In learning how to invest his spiritual capital in a few short years, Matt, an unassuming and straightforward individual, has built a multi-million-dollar Internet marketing and seminar business. He wasn't always so successful. Like many young people, when he graduated from college he had ambitions to make money, start a family, and become financially secure. But he wasn't sure exactly how to do this. His first business, an undercapitalized sales venture, put him so far in debt that eventually he filed for bankruptcy. As he made a fresh start, he vowed to cultivate skills and knowledge that would enable him to do things differently the second time around. He prayed for the right opportunity.

Taking a job with an event-coordination firm that promoted events by leading personal development speakers such as Tony Robbins and Mark Victor Hansen, Matt was exposed to new ideas and life strategies. Along the way, he absorbed a great deal of these teachers' insights and inspiration. Internet marketing was a relatively new tactic in promotion, and it excited him. Although at times he may have had some doubts about himself, he persisted, eventually learning how to market on the Internet by affiliating himself with other individuals who had products to sell. In a few years he realized that it was not only important to share his experience, it was also worth a great deal of money to other entrepreneurs. They could make a lot of money by taking his advice, and he could make a lot of money teaching them. Matt's journey strengthened his faith in his spiritual assets, as well as his belief in Spirit's unseen hands.

In an industry where there are many charismatic teachers, Matt is a low-key alternative. His authenticity and self-effacing humor provide a winning contrast to the slick promises of fast money by Internet marketing courses that lack common sense. His core values and spiritual approach to success are reflected in the way he treats his employees and the courtesy he shows his many students. For example, he offers a free one- to two-hour question-and-answer call-in session every Monday night, and he prides himself in almost never missing a night — even though he might be in Singapore, or down with the flu, or experiencing a power outage.

Matt lives the soul-currency lifestyle. His spiritual partner is his wife, who has both administrative and marketing skills. Their expanding adventureprise has grown from affiliate marketing to a vast array of information products marketed to a growing list of more than a million people. Matt loves what he does, which is to teach others, provide tools, and see prosperity and satisfaction flow in. He is especially grateful for all the people he has had the opportunity to meet, for his family, and for the blessings of success, which are a return for the greater good of serving and benefiting others.

Principle 2. Let Life Lead You

Professional basketball player Dikembe Mutombo exemplifies the principle of letting life lead you. He is one of only a few professional athletes from the Democratic Republic of Congo. Growing up, Mutombo was surrounded by less fortunate friends and village neighbors who contracted and died of many diseases that had already been eradicated in the West. His first goal was to become a doctor and to help treat and find a cure for HIV and AIDS, which are widespread in his native country. A solid high school student, he applied for and received a scholarship from the U.S. Agency for International Development to go to Georgetown University, in Washington, D.C., where he planned to study medicine.

Also Mutombo was 7′2″, a fact not lost on the Georgetown basketball coach, John Thompson Sr., who was famous for finding and developing "big men." He invited Mutombo to join the team, and the young man learned quickly. Mutombo became a legendary shot blocker and defender, leading Georgetown to the top ten in collegiate basketball in the years he played for them. Mutombo was the fourth pick in the 1991 draft of the National Basketball Association, where he became one of the greatest defensive centers ever to play the game. He has played for several teams over an eighteen-year span, and been named an All-Star player four times and Defensive Player of the Year twice. The 42-year-old Mutombo is one of the oldest active players in the NBA and currently plays for the Houston Rockets. Besides his shot-blocking abilities, Mutombo is known for his philanthropic work, which includes serving as spokesperson for the international relief agency CARE.

Part of adventureprise is living life's mystery and letting it lead you through happy accidents and blessings in disguise to the perfect place to fulfill your intentions. Mutombo didn't see himself as a great athlete. All he knew was that he wanted to help people. Becoming a basketball player was an accident that wouldn't have come about if Georgetown hadn't had a medical program that attracted his attention. Then he discovered his love for athletics, which brought him such extraordinary success that he was able to help more people than he had ever imagined he could. That's living in the true flow of soul currency. When you allow your soul to connect you with Spirit, latent talents and capabilities sometimes emerge. As you move to a higher consciousness — multisensory awareness — your spiritual assets are more powerfully invested.

Principle 3. Trust Your Intuition

Cynthia Segal is a perfect example of an individual who activated a latent asset. Growing up in a traditional Jewish family in

Canada, Cynthia followed a mainstream career path, becoming a computer systems analyst working with large and small businesses in Canada and internationally. One day, she saw a demonstration of applied kinesiology (the art of muscle testing to confirm information, intention, or actions). She learned that muscle testing was a physical confirmation of extrasensory information that a part of the mind cannot know. In the class, populated with doctors, healing practitioners, and herself, Cynthia began experiencing extraordinary results, even getting insights beyond the questions she had asked. From muscle testing she moved to energy reading. Then her new interests started to filter into her daily life and she recognized that she had a life purpose other than designing computers.

When she first decided to use her gifts to help people outside her classes, Cynthia often asked, "What words do I use to describe myself and what I do?" Not everyone understood. The greater her skills as an intuitive grew, the greater the chasm between herself and her family and some of her friends became. To say that they could not suspend their belief in the physical/material world in order to support her would be an understatement. Feeling alone and divorced from the world she grew up in, Cynthia stayed on her new path. She saw that her advice changed her clients' lives, setting their minds at peace and giving them clarity about difficult decisions. For the first time in her life, Cynthia was passionate about something.

Today, Cynthia no longer designs computer systems. She is a top medical and personal intuitive who has a special gift for working with energy. She serves corporate chief executive officers and other clients from diverse walks of life. Her appointment book is almost always filled to overflowing, and she frequently appears on radio and TV. Most important, every day is a day she looks forward to, and each client is an opportunity to celebrate service and change lives. Now she has conviction in the power of the unseen that she didn't have before her unexpected gift emerged and changed the course of her life.

As much as soul currency is a state of being that is felt by the heart, it's also activated and directed by thought. Consciousness sets up choices for us. Thought directs our actions. We become the vehicles of Spirit expressing itself without boundary or limitation.

Principle 4. Take Risks, as Anything Is Possible

When you invest your spiritual capital in positive ways, you make a choice to live in a world of possibility rather than limitation and fear. Subconsciously you may gravitate to the exact choices that will help you transcend your conception of limitation and teach you to accept your magnificence. You can find inspirational examples all around you of people doing this every day. By recognizing that the same soul currency is within them that is within you, you can claim their boldness and go-for-it attitude for yourself.

Welshman Paul Potts was working as a salesman in a mobile phone retail store. But one day he trembled as he took what he saw as the biggest risk of his life. He auditioned for the hit show *Britain's Got Talent*. The panel of judges Potts faced included the infamous Simon Cowell, who also appears as a judge on *American Idol*, and whose merciless comments to the acts he finds wanting are legendary; Piers Morgan, another of the original *American Idol* judges; and British TV actress Amanda Holden.

Cowell watched as the slightly overweight, unassuming young man walked to the microphone. "And what are you here for?" he asked, as if the performance was going to be an imposition.

"I'm here to sing opera," Potts replied. With a gap in his front teeth from a motorcycle accident, he hardly reminded anyone of Pavarotti, and his quiet demeanor sharply contrasted with the behavior of many of the previous contestants, who sang rock and roll and pop songs. The judges looked at each other, seemingly wondering if they would have to bear yet another insufferable presentation. Cowell flicked his pen between his fingers, much like a cat twitching its tail in annoyance, as Potts settled himself in.

For Potts, his chance had arrived. He had been moved by music since he was a child, and whenever he felt like he didn't fit in he would go to an isolated place and sing. His voice, as he has described it, was his friend, sometimes his only friend. Several years before the contest, he'd discovered opera. He'd started to take voice lessons, more as a way to strengthen his relationship with his friend than for professional gain. But his job in the mobile phone warehouse was not enough to pay for lessons. That's when a friend told him about the audition.

Paul Potts opened his mouth and began. The energy of his soul, which had been pent up all these years, began to flow out expressively in the words of "Nessun Dorma" ("None Shall Sleep") from Puccini's opera *Turandot*. The judges immediately sat up, surprised. And as Potts continued, the audience began applauding the virtuoso performance, their enthusiasm building until, as he hit the climax of the aria, they spontaneously jumped to their feet, cheering and applauding. The moving performance brought tears to the eyes of Amanda Holden, and even tough-guy Simon Cowell broke into a broad smile of approval.

The rest is history. Potts reprised "Nessun Dorma" again to win the talent search, each time moving audiences with the voice of his soul. His voice, which for so many lonely moments had been his closest friend, now got the attention of Andrea Bocelli. And the dream that Paul Potts finally believed he was worthy to have, took the form of a Sony recording contract and appearances. And yes, a local dentist who witnessed the audition offered to fix Paul's front teeth so that at his later appearances he would be polished and professional. Potts lives the energy of soul currency, as both an inspiration for others and the adventureprise of his soul's expression.

Principle 5. Live Mindfully

Thinking of the tentative beauty of long unexpressed spiritual assets emerging, I am reminded of a spring flower I watched pushing its way through a crack in a New York City sidewalk as I walked to my office. It managed to grow an inch or so amid the smog, concrete boundaries, and heavy foot-traffic, and it even put out a small bud. But one day, just as the bud began to open and be noticeable, a pedestrian crushed it. The lesson here is that we can bloom where we are planted, but some environments are more nurturing than others. If we choose an environment filled by distractions and examples of unconscious living, this is a reflection of our consciousness.

Living mindfully is often described as living in the present moment. It's a way of training your consciousness. As you open to the multisensory world that is inherently you, introspection — going within — is one of the most important channels for bringing the inner Spirit into harmony with the creative intention that your mind craves.

It's easiest to connect with your essence during meditation. Buddhist masters tell the story of a man seeking enlightenment who gets on a horse galloping down the road. "Where are you going?" asks a bystander. The man on the horse replies, "Only the horse knows." The illustration means for you to bring your thoughts into accord with your soul, so that intention is your state of being, and your thoughts flow harmoniously and lovingly.

Have you observed that your most inspiring ideas may come when you're engaged in activities that allow you to clear your mind? Without taking quiet time, your mind might be too cluttered to receive pure intuition and guidance. I know inventors who get their best ideas when they are on the toilet or taking a shower. One chief executive officer gets his greatest inspiration by gazing out his picture window at the quiet solitude of the lake in back of his home. Runners and swimmers experience athleticism as a form of moving meditation, as do practitioners of tai chi chuan, who say that in the mindful flow of movement they become one with their mind.

More often than not, less is more. Simplicity does not mean renouncing the world and going into a monastery. It means allowing your soul currency to flow without adding busyness. There is depth and richness of complexity in simplicity, while in busyness there is just activity, wasted energy, and emotional disconnection from inner wisdom. In simplicity there is certainty; in busyness there is the fallacy that more activity means a greater certainty of success. Simplicity elevates states of consciousness.

It's easier to create the presence of mindfulness when the television is not always on, and when your intentionality is to live with love, compassion, nonjudgment, and encouragement. You take on the energy of what's around you. If you've ever watched *Touched by an Angel* or *Seventh Heaven*, compare how you feel when tuning in to a televised exhibition of the Ultimate Fighting Championship or *CSI: Miami*. Notice how your body changes. A camera using Kirlian photography would pick up instantaneous changes in your body's energy field. The colors and dimensions of your aura would change. When you're trying to be mindful in an atmosphere of violent TV programs, conflict, or noisy energy, it's a lot like bathing in dirty water. You go through the motions of bathing, but you never get clean.

Mindfulness is easier in an environment of support and love, such as when you're around people who are positive, empowering, and cheerful — especially friends and family. By setting your intention to be loved and supported, you'll find that difficult people begin to drop away.

Listen to your body's response to living mindfully. This form of soul currency reduces stress, lowers blood pressure, and contributes overall to better health. Mindfulness meditation has been shown to reduce pain as well as the diseases associated with old age. In the late 1970s, Dr. Jon Kabat-Zinn began using meditation at the University of Massachusetts Medical Center's Stress Reduction Clinic in Worcester. There are now over a hundred similar hospital-based programs throughout the United States, including one near me at Holy Cross Hospital in Fort Lauderdale, Florida, which has its own mind-body medicine coordinator.[1]

Most recently, the Institute of HeartMath in Boulder Creek, California, conducted extensive research showing that good health starts with love, and that love can reduce stress.[2] Quick, simple exercises, such as reimagining a cherished memory, can significantly improve your health when done on a regular basis. The institute's clients include companies such as Hewlett-Packard, Shell, Unilever, Cisco Systems, and Boeing. The institute has developed a consistent track record helping managers and employees to decrease stress and increase joy in their lives and work.

Principle 6. Remember Your Essence

Remember, you are first an energy being, linked to the cosmos by soul currency, and second a human being in a body. Often people are unwilling to remember this, especially if they've lapsed into self-cherishing consciousness. We give our centers of power to people or events outside us, which appear to be beyond our control.

We judge ourselves on what others think of us. We attach our self-worth to the outcome of any project, goal, or decision.

Experiments done by the Institute for Research on Unlimited Love, founded by Dr. Stephen G. Post, confirm the benefits of giving, kindness, and compassion on the giver's health and well-being as much as on the recipient's.[3] Imagine starting the day in harmony and empowerment by giving or receiving a compliment, hugging a friend or loved one, or simply enjoying a playful smile or laugh. Now imagine what it would be like if you started the same day by having a nasty argument with your neighbor.

One tribal tradition in Africa states that, when an individual has committed a crime or has engaged in an antisocial act that goes against tribal law, the offender must be seated in the center of the square in full view of everyone in the tribe. One by one, all tribe members come up to the offender and speak to him or her about what they remember best about the good he or she has done. Each person relates his or her own experience of a good deed, kind act, or even an encouraging word remembered about the offender. No matter how long it takes, each person in the village comes up to the offender to remind the offender of the goodness within him or her.

We all need to be reminded about how magnificent we are. We sometimes take a kind word or a good deed for granted. But without an encouraging word, we may have no idea about what a difference we have made in another's life. Only through connection with others are we reminded. And in that reminder, we know that Spirit is both speaking to us and knowing itself through us. Indeed, Spirit is always magnificent; it's only the separation that we feel at times that requires us to be reminded.

If you're wondering what all this has to do with prosperity, remember that love is the raw source-material of the universe. An exercise such as this activates the circulation of soul currency and raises consciousness to match the higher vibration of love. Then the "reality" around us changes to harmonize with the higher frequency of energy. There really is nothing to *do* when it comes to loving or forgiving. There is only something to remember. We remember and open to our magnificence, abundance, and love.

Principle 7. Practice Proactive Gratitude

Be present with gratitude. Thankfulness for being the loving energy you are is an indication that you've moved beyond the self-cherishment stage into recognition of your connectedness to something greater. So give thanks for already having received what you envision. Affirm that you are open and focused on your highest and best choices. Although you might have been taught that gratitude is an acknowledgment that occurs *after* something happens, in a multisensory world there is only the present. By being proactive in your gratitude, you focus on the now, not simply on what has happened in the past. When you live in soul currency, you focus on and believe in receiving good. You live in a divine creative space where dreams are fulfilled through attraction and intention.

Being present with gratitude also provides a means to bring your feelings about money and prosperity into the divine creative space, away from the negative emotions you once attached to needing money. By opening up to gratitude, you lovingly acknowledge that Spirit is the only source of your supply. In gratitude, you recognize your true prosperity: the blessings of the presence and circulation of love in your relationships, the flow of opportunities, the people who come into your life, your health and well-being, and much more.

I learned a deep appreciation for the power of gratitude through my acquaintance with João de Deus, the Brazilian healer. My intention when I first visited his healing center, Casa de Dom

Inácio, was to support a young friend who earlier had been in a car accident and suffered severe spinal injuries. She was paralyzed from the chest down, and because her spinal cord had been crushed, doctors felt she was lucky to be alive. After a number of trips to Brazil, she had improved slowly and was now ready to stand up for the first time since her accident. I knew of the selfless work that this healer had done for her, and I was thrilled to have the opportunity to meet him. In addition, a very slow-growing lipoma (a fatty tumor) near my spine was beginning to worry me.

The entire visit was life-changing. I was deeply moved as I watched my friend rise with some difficulty from her chair and stand on her own with the help of braces. I saw the hope and gratitude that her previous visits had given her. Moreover, I saw that instead of focusing on the tragedy, she was affirming life — not only her own but also the lives of all those around her. When it was my turn, the healer asked me to turn around so he could look at the lipoma. Then he said in Portuguese, "Tomorrow physical spiritual intervention."

Back in her wheelchair, my friend asked me if I was nervous. I said that while I had been at the healing center, I had watched several videotapes of others with bigger lipomas than mine having similar spiritual interventions. There were two forms of spiritual intervention: the physical kind of healing that looked like surgery, and the less visible energetic healing. But the videos I saw of what appeared to be an incision and the removal of the tumor with forceps and a scalpel involved no apparent pain and no blood, and the intervention was over in minutes. So my intuition told me that I had come to the right place, no matter that logic and appearances said otherwise.

The next day, as I was lying face-down waiting to have the lipoma removed, I remembered that it was Thanksgiving back home. How ironic, I thought, that I was getting twenty-five years of stuck energy (in the form of the lipoma) taken off my back. The metaphor was clear to me. The physical spiritual intervention took only minutes. The process was videotaped and closely watched by a Brazilian Canadian naturopath who would review it with me later. After finishing, the healer showed me the pieces of the tumor, which would have filled a small coffee cup.

I felt great and was impatient to get up and leave. The naturopath stopped by my bed and told me I had been most fortunate: One of the tendrils of the tumor had wrapped around my vertebral artery, which in a few years would have resulted in my being confined to a wheelchair. Parts of the tumor had become engaged with the spine itself, and he said that it was unlikely that any hospital in the United States or Canada would have taken on the liability of a surgical procedure in which even the tiniest nick could result in paralysis.

Since that time, each day when I get up I am grateful I can walk without pain, play tennis with joy, and run along the lake during sunset. Through my healing experience, I learned to live in proactive gratitude, the expectancy of good. I am unattached to how events look, as I have learned not to put limits on how Spirit chooses to enrich my life.

Proactive gratitude involves trust. When you trust Spirit, you're able to create a life of rich possibilities. So when you practice mindfulness during the day, focus on everything you're grateful for. When you fail to give thanks for the abundance of life, you actually limit what is available to you. When you complain about what you don't have, rather than give thanks for what you have, you attract more of the same: in other words, not enough. Here are four practices that will help you live in a state of proactive gratitude:

- Focus on the good in your life. We've been so conditioned to be aware of what we need or what is wrong. Instead, focus on what's good in your life, what you already have, and what you have that you can give to life. You're already rich beyond your wildest dreams.

- Make gratitude a conscious habit. Change the way you think and talk about your life. Don't minimize your accomplishments or your abilities. Try this exercise: For an entire day, write down two things every hour that you did right in that hour, and pat yourself on the back. If you were kind, praise yourself as if you were praising someone else. Your subconscious hears this, and in the process you change your beliefs about yourself. Your soul accepts this praise as love, and your self-love becomes God-love.

- Share your good. Sharing is a natural way of affirming your good and recognizing that good flows through you, not just to you. As good flows through you, it raises your consciousness of connectedness to Spirit. Share your good by sharing the positive feelings of having good, rather than the negative stories or feelings of the past. Share abundance by looking for opportunities to give and serve others.

- Surrender. Surrendering to gratitude is seeing the blessing in whatever happens and whatever choices you have to make. Surrender also consists of being guided to the highest and best choices for you and acknowledging that Spirit is expressing itself through you and as you. When we are grateful, we surrender our ego. When we surrender to gratitude, we return our concept of ego to Spirit and replace it with trust, love, and openness to receiving good.

Principle 8. Remember That Work Should Be Fun

In learning to live in soul currency, don't forget that life, service, and work can be filled with joy and fun. The ability to laugh is a special gift. It takes us out of the thinking mind and reminds us of our humanness. Laughter is so healing that Dr. Patch Adams made it the mission of his medical practice. He dressed as a clown, delighting young children and making older children (ages ten to one hundred) laugh. After his mother had a serious operation, Adams remembered, "My mother had a below-knee amputation as a result of having diabetes and smoking all of her life. When she was regaining consciousness in the Recovery Unit, I smiled at her and said, 'Well mum, how does it feel to have one leg in the grave?' She laughed out loud. Till the day she died, she told that story to her friends, and each time, she laughed again."[4]

Adams opened the way for others to incorporate laughter into healing. Dr. Shayne Yates, from Melbourne, Australia, and his wife, Patricia Cameron-Hill, a nurse, teach seminars on how to bring more laughter into hospitals, because, as they say, "No one has a monopoly on humor." They call their seminars "Outbreaks of Joy," explaining, "If you're a patient, or visitor, or health care worker, there are many ways you can lighten the hospital experience."[5]

One suggestion, offered long ago by the legendary Norman Cousins, who laughed his way to recovery when he was diagnosed with a terminal illness, is to give patients access to comedy shows and uplifting stories. Another is to present patients with humorous buttons, such as a badge reading, "Under repair, please handle with care," or to hang up a sign in the patient's room saying, "Any place that serves breakfast in bed can't be all that bad." Or post cartoons, such as a psychiatrist's advertisement, "Satisfaction guaranteed, or your mania back" or "A hypochondriac is a person who can read the doctor's prescription." Or hand the patient a hospital-gown safety pin that reads, "For hospital gown gaposis — because the front is rated G and the back is rated R!"[6]

Dance, music, and art are expressions of soul currency. Anyone who has ever watched ballet productions by George Balanchine or Twyla Tharp will know that these expressions bring us into a deep soul connection. When you choose to express this individually in dancing, at first you may feel conscious of your steps and how you look. Then you and your partner will begin dancing together, conscious only of moving as one. Ultimately it becomes an experience of joy in greater consciousness — learning to dance as one with the beloved Divine. The term *whirling dervishes* came from sacred Sufi dancing, an integral part of mystical Islam. Dancing is a metaphor for experiencing your soul as fun.

Music has the ability to connect you with your soul. It stirs emotion and even changes the body's vibration. But music is as diverse as our moods and as the people playing it. So discover what music inspires you, what instruments make you introspective, and what music makes you flow. Choose to surround yourself with the music that not only makes you relax and feel good but also stirs positive emotions, makes you feel alive, and encourages you to become the greater you.

Principle 9. Love What You Do

To live in soul currency is to recognize that you are a multisensory energy being that is connected to, and expressing, the source energy of creation. This greater concept of yourself allows you to choose whether to be stuck in the material world of powerlessness over conditions, or to embrace the power of your soul currency. By accepting your enormous gifts as a multisensory being, you can learn to live from possibility and intention, rather than fear.

Mo Siegel, one of the founders of the herbal tea giant Celestial Seasonings, picked herbs and berries in his backyard and in the Colorado mountains. His curiosity that some of the herbs he picked might help his asthma led him to develop a passion for making tea.[7] Legendary herbologist Hanna Kroeger once related to me how Siegel and his Celestial cofounder, Wyck Hay, would pick herbs and sell them to her herbal shop in Boulder. She would often brew herbal tea for her customers, something that Siegel also did when he opened a small art gallery and health food store soon afterward.

From humble beginnings and a well-developed taste for herbal tea, Celestial Seasonings was born. Initially, Siegel and Wyck ran the company out of their store in an old barn and their homes, with their wives and friends hand-sewing tea bags. They gave the teas imaginative names. Red Zinger, a blend of hibiscus, rosehips, and lemongrass, was the company's first major product and even today is one of its best sellers. Little did Mo Siegel dream that a passion for tea would ignite the herbal tea industry.

When, like Siegel and his partners, you find a catalyst for your passion, have the courage to recognize it. Do something with it that no one else is doing. Tea making, for example, was more than two thousand years old, but Celestial Seasonings revolutionized the industry by offering herb teas for pleasure that previously had been used for medical purposes only. Develop a profit path. Siegel sold premium teas with high profit margins. By fiscal year 2000, the few dollars and the spiritual capital Siegel and his partners had initially invested were worth more than $100 million in annual sales. That year, the company merged with organic food giant Hain Food Group in a $390 million transaction.[8] Invest your spiritual capital with purpose and wisdom in the adventureprise of your soul.

No matter how crowded the market may seem, you can bring unique value to it. Seth Goldman started the Honest Tea Company out of his kitchen with a thermos in 1998. Goldman, who at the time was in business school, liked to play pickup basketball. He was in search of the perfect thirst-quenching beverage. Most were too sweet or too tasteless. After years spent concocting different combinations of juices and flavors, he contacted his old business-school professor who had just returned from India, where he'd been analyzing the tea industry. Among the many things he told Seth was that most of the tea used by American companies was lower quality dust and what the industry called "fannings," which were left over lower quality tea leaves. Out of the many hours and the significant spiritual capital Seth invested in his project, the adventureprise of Honest Tea took shape. He brought thermoses of tea and a bottle with a mock label to a presentation to buyers at Fresh Fields (now part of Whole Foods Markets).[9] The store's buyers connected with Seth's vision and story. Their first order was for fifteen thousand bottles, which Seth confidently assured them he could deliver even though he had yet to figure out the logistics of producing that much tea or to find the right bottling facility. But with an order in hand, he found the right vendors.

"Doing Business Differently" is the company's motto, and we can see why. Honest Tea is Fair Trade–certified. It is organic. The company has developed revenue-sharing partnerships with supplier communities in South Africa, India, and the Crow Reservation in Montana. A portion of its sales have gone to nonprofits such as the Pretty Shield Foundation for at-risk Native American youth and City Year, an AmeriCorps program that unites diverse young people with communities in need.

Muriel Strode, in *At the Roots of Grasses*, has written, "Do not go where the path may lead, go instead where there is no path and leave a trail."[10] There are more opportunities to express yourself today. Invest your spiritual capital in what is uniquely yours to do, whether the profit path is buying and developing real estate, as Donald Trump did, developing a better tattoo machine, creating a new social network, or following other passions that stir your imagination or can be lots of fun. Retire the belief that you can't possibly be well paid to do something that you might even do for free. New markets are being created daily, and there are more opportunities to create your own work than ever before. Not only are you looking for opportunity, opportunity is all around you today and looking for you.

Be clear about your purpose and mission as you blaze a trail. Your enterprise in life will become the enterprise of your soul, as has happened for notables such as Seth Goldman of Honest Tea, Steve Jobs of Apple, and Ben Cohen of Ben & Jerry's. Your spiritual capital will help create the investors who will be drawn to the greater idea of your vision. Recognize the connectedness between your thought and intention, and in your journey allow your soul currency to create and enrich you in all senses. You have the inner tools for success, and the great not-so-silent support of the spiritual universe, which will appear to reorganize itself to support you. Live from a sense of fun, a determination of purpose, and the joy of doing what really fulfills you. Know that every step you take is a building block to greater flows of financial and spiritual enrichment. May this be your beginning.

EXERCISES FOR YOUR SOUL

The following three exercises will help you live in the flow.

MANAGING YOUR SPIRITUAL PORTFOLIO

Observe Your Personal Flow

Traffic is a metaphor for how things flow in the material world. Driving can bring up both negative emotions such as annoyance, judgment, fear, and anger, and positive emotions such as kindness and compassion. Once in a while, the journey seems effortless. Although there may be traffic and stoplights, the journey you experience is one in which time seems to stop and you arrive easily at your destination. In the next few days, observe your inner experience of going to and from work, school, or any other destination in a car. (Note: If you are an urban dweller or someone who uses mass transportation, please translate this exercise into language appropriate for your circumstances. Foot traffic and bus and subway travel offer opportunities to study flow as much as car travel does.)

Are you present to the flow of the journey, or do you look at it as just a way to get to a destination? Notice if you're relaxed or tense and how this affects your experience. Do any external circumstances, such as being on time or weather conditions, affect the flow of your drive? Do you see yourself as connected at all to other drivers on the road, or do you have a "me versus them" attitude? When it comes to finding a parking space at your destination, do you flow into it, or is it a struggle?

Jot down your experiences for several days, and then take a quiet moment and review them with love and mindfulness. Give thanks and bless the experience.

PERSONAL EXPERIENCE

Create a Vision of Total Flow in Your Future

Imagine that thirty-six months have passed since reading this book. Describe how you have used your spiritual capital, your connection to your stakeholders, and the creative energy of love in the following areas:

1. The work and service you do:
2. Your financial flow:

3. Elimination of counterfeit beliefs (be specific):

4. Your spiritual awareness:

5. Your happiness and fulfillment:

MEDITATION

Practice Forgiveness and All-Encompassing Love

Prosperous flow comes from love. Experience the soul currency of love in a new way, as a feeling of deep well-being. As you sit quietly, focus on the energy area around the heart (the heart chakra). As you take two deep, cleansing breaths, imagine that the energy of your heart now totally surrounds you. You see this as a white light that feels wonderfully soothing. Now, focus on your breath. Watch as your energy expands, and become aware of how it merges into the universal field of love.

Allow yourself to truly love yourself by focusing this energy inward. Perhaps for too long your focus has been on being loving to others. Now remember yourself. As you focus your energy inward, remember that the essence of your energy is Spirit. In this quiet moment, allow yourself to forgive anything you may have done in the past or that you believe you should have done but did not. Now imagine the universal field of loving energy welling up through you, saturating every part of your visible and invisible being, and spreading out to eternity and then back through you.

ACKNOWLEDGMENTS

This book might not have been published without the help of Stephanie Gunning, my publishing consultant, who helped shape the book proposal and who assisted in the creation of the final manuscript. She was a wonderful sounding board and was indispensable. Thanks also to Mark Victor Hansen, whose Mega Book Marketing Conference inspired me and led me to educational resources; and to Cheryl Harrison, who designed my web page, gave me hands-on support in developing an image for the Soul Currency Institute, and was the best alter ego I could ever have. I am grateful to Stephany Evans, my literary agent at Fine Print Literary Management, who placed the book with the perfect publisher and walked me through the publishing process. For her wonderful editor's eye, I am thankful to Georgia Hughes at New World Library. Much appreciation also goes to Bonita Hurd for her detailed copyediting.

Special acknowledgment goes to my friends and colleagues Dr. Arleen Bump, senior pastor of the Center for Spiritual Living in Fort Lauderdale, Florida, and Reverend James Lockard, copastor of the Westlake Church of Religious Science in California, for their encouragement and support in developing my spiritual abundance material. I feel exceptionally blessed to have taken a special one-week class at the feet of the Dalai Lama, whose ideas on enlightenment, love, and kindness have found their way into this book. And I acknowledge my friend João de Deus (also known as John of God) and the many compassionate spirits who helped me experience the soul's real currency of love.

A warm thank-you goes to all my dearest friends and mentors who endorsed this work in its early stages: Cary Bayer; Deepak Chopra, MD; Alan Cohen; Barbara De Angelis, PhD; John DeMartini, DC; John Gray, PhD; John Harricharan; Jean Houston, PhD; Jason Oman; and many others. I gratefully acknowledge the help of Randy Denton for his assistance in bringing this book to Dr. Chopra's attention, Kelly Gallagher for her warm introduction to Dr. Gray, and Bob Stein for arranging for me to meet Dr. Houston. Deep special thanks also go to Joel Spector for his ongoing sage advice, Joel Roberts for helping me clarify my message, Matt Bacak for opening up the world of Internet marketing and for his encouragement, Alex Mandossian for teaching me about teleseminars, and Gary Zukav and Linda Francis for instilling in me the consciousness of authentic power, which was so important in writing this book.

I gratefully acknowledge my many students who have taught me more than I can even express, as well as the many fellow authors and friends who have encouraged me along the way, including Diane Cirincione, PhD; Sandy Grason; Marie Heiland; Diane Hom; Richard Israel; Donna LeBlanc, M.Ed.; Candy Paull; Elisabeth Rossen; Cynthia Segal; Terry Shintani, MD, JP, MPH; and Maureen Whitehouse. And thanks to Andrea Napoleon, who has been more of a teacher than she will ever know. Finally, I am grateful to my Amherst College freshman English professor, Dr. Robert "Kim" Townsend, whose encouragement has stuck with me all these decades, and to my longtime friend Doug Russell, who first started me on the path of writing books, more than thirty years ago.

PRAYER

I Am the Source of Eternal Flow

Knowing that there is one eternal source of all love and divine supply, I know that my life is that one life, and that all supply and abundance are now mine. As I fully open to receive them, I am open to the creative energies of love flowing as fulfillment, and to creativity manifesting as successful projects and grand prosperity. No longer do I allow doubt and unworthiness to be a part of me, for I now know the truth, that I am Spirit manifest, and that I am capable of cocreating and directing a life full of love, flowing with joyfulness and surplus. I am abundantly self-sufficient in all my needs, and I live from the higher truth of being in the work and service that are mine to do, and in loving interactions with all whose lives I touch.

Giving thanks — for it is gratitude that connects us to and reminds us of our God nature — and knowing that my words have power and are already working in my life, I release this into the universal presence.

And so it is.

PERSONAL FINANCIAL BALANCE SHEET

ASSETS		LIABILITIES	
CURRENT ASSETS		CURRENT LIABILITIES	
Cash and equivalents	_____	Payables	_____
Stocks, bonds,		Short-term debt	
and securities	_____	*(under one year)*	_____
Short-term receivables	_____	SUBTOTAL CURRENT	
Other	_____	LIABILITIES	_____
SUBTOTAL CURRENT			
ASSETS	_____		
OTHER ASSETS		OTHER LIABILITIES	
Real estate	_____	Bank debt	
Other investments		*(over one year)*	_____
(nonliquid)	_____	Notes	_____
Personal effects	_____	Contingent liabilities	_____
Equipment *(including*		SUBTOTAL OTHER	
auto) and fixtures	_____	LIABILITIES	_____
Collectibles, art,			
and so on	_____		
SUBTOTAL OTHER ASSETS	_____	**TOTAL LIABILITIES**	_____
SUBTOTAL SPIRITUAL ASSETS		**NET WORTH***	_____
(from exercise)	_____		
		TOTAL LIABILITIES	
TOTAL ASSETS	_____	**+ NET WORTH**	_____

% Tangible assets**/total assets _____%
(What percentage of your total assets are your tangible assets?)

% Spiritual assets/total assets _____%
(What percentage of your total assets are your spiritual assets?)

* Net worth = total assets − total liabilities
** Tangible assets = subtotal current assets + subtotal other assets

SUGGESTIONS FOR
SOUL CURRENCY
STUDY GROUPS

A *Soul Currency* book study group combines many of the aspects of a mastermind group[1] with a soul currency class. Among other things, it's an opportunity to set intentionality as a group and to bond as a small community. Such a group should not be undertaken lightly, any more than a prayer or mastermind group would be. Joining a book study group is a commitment to be responsible for your own growth, as well as to see and to hold the intention for the highest and best in life to manifest for each person in the group.

When you set up a *Soul Currency* book study group, the members may choose to mutually adopt the following commitments to one another:

1. We create a safe space and agree to hold everything that's said in confidence.

2. We commit to open and authentic communication. For example, if any of us will be late or must miss a meeting, that person will take responsibility for letting the rest of the group know.

3. We commit to showing up — and not just physically. This means we commit to reading the material beforehand and preparing for the next meeting, being on time, and participating fully in discussions.

4. We commit to loving and appreciative conversation, and to sharing from the heart without hidden agendas.

5. We agree that the meeting should begin with either a centering time for quiet meditation or a centering prayer, or both.

6. We will set a time for the group to adjourn, and set our intentions for the week either through prayer or through silence before we conclude.

SETTING UP THE GROUP

Here are some additional suggestions:

1. Choose an appropriate venue to meet, such as a home or other meeting place that is quiet and enables confidentiality, a place where your group won't be interrupted. Also, taking an occasional break to have water, tea, or other beverages and light snacks is a good idea.

2. Agree on whether you will have an open or closed group. An open group permits the addition of new members as you go along, and a closed group does not. I've found that either one can work, and that the success of any group depends on having committed participants.

3. Leadership and facilitation roles should be rotated among group members.

4. A larger group (more than seven) allows for greater discussion and more points of view, but typically not everyone will get to speak. A more intimate group enables more complete interaction.

COURSE OF STUDY

I recommend that you take the opportunity to hold one discussion meeting per chapter. During the last half hour of the meeting, do the exercises at the ends of the chapters. Try to meet weekly or biweekly, depending on the participants' schedules. Other considerations:

1. Each person should come prepared to share what happened to him or her during the week and explain how it applied to what he or she learned.

2. Devote one meeting to a review after the third chapter, "Your Spiritual Capital," and after the seventh chapter, "Soul Currency 'Magic.'" This means that the group will meet at least nine times. Participants will experience a great deal of progress during this nine-week period.

3. Participants should go to the readers-only section of the SoulCurrency.org website to download new information or forms or get answers for questions relating to the group.

4. You may choose to share the book with a family member or business associate. If you do so, this will produce between the two of you a common understanding of the concepts of creating abundance and flow.

GENERAL PRINCIPLES FOR
GROUP DISCUSSION

Having facilitated numerous study groups throughout my career, I find it worth mentioning the following few principles that typically help interactions run smoothly:

1. There should be an agreement prior to each class about the length of individual discussion, so that everyone has an opportunity to participate.

2. The facilitator should make a handout of the four or five key ideas of the chapter to be discussed. Such handouts need not be fancy. Each week's leader should be responsible for preparing that particular week's handout.

3. The leader should make it a point to facilitate involvement and encourage contributions from less-outspoken participants.

4. Especially meaningful excerpts from the book might be read aloud to start a discussion or make a point.

5. Participants should endeavor to give examples from their own lives if these examples are truly relevant to the point being made.

I also invite you and your group's other participants to join the soul currency community interest group on the web to exchange personal postings, take a class, attend a weekend event, and become a member of the Soul Currency Institute's coaching program to get the most out of your learning experience.

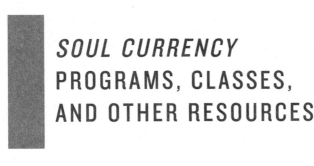

SOUL CURRENCY
PROGRAMS, CLASSES,
AND OTHER RESOURCES

Never again say, "I don't have anything of value to contribute." Remember how much you bring to life, and the enormous number of people you have already helped. Let your life sparkle with love and richness, fulfillment and abundance. To assist your progress, and to provide greater support than you can get from this book alone, I've created the following programs, which you can sign up for on my website (www.soulcurrency.org).

SOUL CURRENCY WEEKENDS

Have a hands-on experience as you learn to open up to the richness of your inner wealth. Discover the principles of how to truly create and invest your spiritual capital. Become the spiritual chief executive officer of your own life, and use the adventureprise of your soul to create fulfillment and prosperity. Put into practice the five steps of soul currency.

SOUL CURRENCY CLASSES

Sign up for online classes that teach different facets of what is covered in this book: "How to Create Prosperity from Your Inner

Wealth," "Your Spiritual Capital: 5 Powerful Ways to Invest," and "Adventureprise." These courses are for beginners, intermediates, and those who have achieved a level of mastery in creating and operating existing businesses. Course offerings change periodically, and we occasionally offer in-person, local classes as well.

COACHING PROGRAM

Join my coaching program and learn how to integrate soul currency into your life. My staff of certified coaches and I will help you eliminate the counterfeit currency in your life and support you in making wise investments of your spiritual assets and capital. Join an empowering and loving community and create fulfillment, joy, and prosperity. I have created a two-year certification program for those interested in teaching others about soul currency; the second year consists of a hands-on program of assisting and teaching classes.

SOUL CURRENCY CD RESOURCES

The basic soul currency course, meditations, and insights into adventureprise and raising capital are available on CD. The basic course will take you through the five steps and teach you to more effectively unleash your soul currency. Resources such as meditations and in-depth interviews with me will help you succeed in turning your inner wealth into outer prosperity.

SOUL CURRENCY "INNERVIEWS"

These "innerviews" are with people just like you who have mastered soul currency. Learn how these experts have taken action, and how their visions, habits, and tools can support you. Seeing how others have applied soul currency will bring your experience of this book to life and stir you to include these experts' methods in your own life and vision for the future.

SOUL CURRENCY KEYNOTE AND PROGRAM SPEECHES

In more than two decades of appearances as a keynote and program speaker, I've found that my presentations have a transformative and empowering effect on individuals, companies, and organizations. The results have been measurable, lasting, and inspirational. The message of soul currency is at the heart of business, entrepreneurship, and the adventureprise of life, and it encourages each of us to become more than we already are. If you'd like to include a soul currency keynote address at an upcoming event, please contact me through www.soul currency.org.

SPECIAL EVENTS

I offer a variety of special events, such as the "Soul Currency and Adventureprise Immersion" event, which are weeklong intensives, or boot camps. As you experience the process of immersion, your counterfeit beliefs can drop away, and lasting change can occur. Other special events, such as trips to China, India, and other countries in Asia, link soul currency with sacred Eastern traditions.

FREE SOUL CURRENCY RESOURCES AT WWW.SOULCURRENCY.ORG/READERS

Congratulations. You have chosen to cultivate soul currency, and you will create greater fulfillment and abundance each day if you put into practice the insights you've gained from this book. Now it's time to reward yourself with the additional gifts I've created to support you in achieving your goals.

- A free downloadable audio recording, *Seven Spiritual Secrets of Financial Giants.* Some of the most successful men and women enjoyed what they did so much that they would have worked for free. Listen to these inspiring stories of success, and learn how these financial giants created what they did.
- A free readers-only downloadable workbook containing all the soul currency exercises, a special self-evaluation soul-currency questionnaire, and other bonus material.
- A free downloadable meditation on prosperity, set to music. This meditation will enable you to make soul currency a daily practice in your life.
- A free year's subscription to the Soul Currency Institute's monthly ezine, filled with evocative articles, insights, and inspiration.
- Access to readers-only free teleseminars with special guests and topics of interest.
- A downloadable readers-only "My Inner Wealth Blossoms" collectible poster. This beautiful image and affirmation can be framed or mounted. Post it to remind yourself of your inner wealth and spiritual capital.

For these and other gifts, please visit
www.soulcurrency.org/readers.

To access these free gifts, readers must provide their first name and email address (these are never shared, rented, or sold). Offer subject to availability.

NOTES

CHAPTER 1. THE FLOW OF SOUL CURRENCY

1. You can read more about Richard Shulman at www.richheartmusic.com.

2. Ernest Holmes, *The Science of Mind* (New York: Dodd, Mead & Company, 1938), pp. 35, 38.

3. Ibid., p. 33.

4. In 2006 the Bureau of Labor Statistics of the U.S. Department of Labor found that the average person spends 9.3 hours working, 7.6 hours sleeping, 3.0 hours pursuing leisure activities, and .09 hours doing household chores. The remaining 3.2 hours of the day might be spent doing any of the above. From the Bureau of Labor Statistics website, www.bls.gov/news.release/atus.nro.htm (accessed May 2, 2008). Entrepreneurs, who generally constitute one in four persons in the workplace, typically work more than five days a week and may work more than ten hours per day. Exact statistics are difficult to come by, but my experience is that, when I worked for myself, I worked more hours.

5. There is not a unified set of statistics that cover all categories of small businesses together with unincorporated full- and part-time self-employed persons. Here are the key statistics: the U.S. Small Business Administration in 2006 estimated there were 25.8 million small businesses. IDC, a leading market research company, in 2005 reported 34.9 million home offices, 18.8 to 20.3 million of which were revenue producing, with the remainder set up for telecommuting or other purposes.

6. The Conference Board (www.conferenceboard.org) is a ninety-year-old, highly regarded, business-supported, nonprofit research organization best known for its Consumer Confidence Index and its Index of Leading Economic Indicators. A February 2005 survey conducted for the Conference Board by TNS, a leading market research company, showed that 50 percent of respondents (down from 60 percent the year before) were satisfied with their jobs. Only 14 percent responded that they were very satisfied (I used this statistic). In addition, the survey found that 25 percent of people take their jobs simply to get a paycheck. Only one-third of the people were satisfied with what they were paid. Biggest job satisfaction declines were registered in the age group 35–54 and among people earning $25,000–$50,000.

7. Sixty-seven percent of American families live paycheck to paycheck. American Payroll Association website, www.accountingweb.com.

8. I found the Studs Terkel quotation on the website www.answers.com, and I originally thought it must have come from the book *Working: People Talk about What They Do All Day and How They Feel about What They Do* (New York: New Press, 1997). However, I have not located the actual citation in the book. It might instead have been drawn from a talk he gave.

9. The quote from Buddha is commonly used in a practice called *metta* meditation, or loving-kindness meditation, in which you wish good health, happiness, and freedom to all beings, including your enemy and yourself. I found it on the website www.opendharma.org, and although I am not certain of the original source, I believe it's one of the best-known Buddhist sutras.

10. Joseph Campbell with Bill Moyers, *The Power of Myth* (New York: Random House, 1988), p. 150.

CHAPTER 2. SPIRITUAL ASSETS

Epigraph: This quotation is often erroneously attributed to Ralph Waldo Emerson, Oliver Wendell Holmes, or Henry David Thoreau. In fact, the author is unknown.

1. Much of the information about the Golconda Diamond Mine appears on the Project Gutenberg website (www.gutenberg.org), an online database of seventeen thousand books whose copyrights are in the public domain in the United States.

2. The statistics on the $1-billion equivalents come from a variety of sources. In about 1996, when my offices were in Trump Tower on Fifth Avenue in Manhattan, I asked the building management what it was worth and was told approximately $300 million. A 2005 eBay listing of the F-16 fighter plane indicated that it would cost $16 million fully assembled and flight-tested, and there would be a $4 million discount if it came unassembled. Later on, I read that the U.S. Department of Homeland Security demanded that the plane's owner and eBay remove the ad. Financial value of the Harry Potter brand is a dynamic figure. You could track book earnings by examining the stock of Scholastic, Inc., the book's American publisher, but that estimation doesn't take into account the income generated by movies, DVDs, and four hundred ancillary products. I estimate someone could buy a majority interest for $4 billion. The organization Feed the Children (www.feedthechildren.org) states, "Just $8 will feed a hungry child for an entire month." At the time of this book's writing, I estimate that there are 100 million children in West Africa.

3. Information about Deborah Weidenhamer and her company comes from Auction Systems Auctioneers and Appraiser, www.auctionandappraise.com, and a phone interview with her.

4. In a memorable commencement address given by Steve Jobs at Stanford University on June 4, 2005, he noted that Reed College offered the best calligraphy instruction in the country. A transcript of this inspiring speech can be found at www.freepublic.com.

5. Keith Ferrazzi and Tahl Raz, *Never Eat Lunch Alone* (New York: Currency/Doubleday, 2005), p. 8.

6. See Gavin Menzies, *1421: The Year the Chinese Discovered America* (New York: HarperCollins, 2003). Menzies's book has been attacked by some scholars primarily because of his background as a retired submarine captain, and the evidence he presents has often been dismissed as speculative or unverified.

CHAPTER 3. YOUR SPIRITUAL CAPITAL

1. Two authors who have written informative books about the subject of causality are David Bohm, *Causality and Chance in Modern Physics* (Princeton, NJ: D. Van Nostrand Company, 1957); and Amit Goswami, *The Self-Aware Universe* (New York: Putnam, 1993).

2. Dr. Masaru Emoto details his Thank Water project on www.hado.net.
3. Peter Senge, C. Otto Sharmer, Betty Sue Flowers, Joseph Jaworski, *Presence: An Exploration of Profound Change in People, Organizations, and Society* (New York: Doubleday Business, 2005), p. 11.
4. Jim Rohn, *The Treasury of Quotes* (Southlake, TX: Jim Rohn International, 1994), p. 37.
5. Mother Teresa, quoted at http://home.att.net/~hillcrestbaptist/mt.html.
6. See *Bio/tech News* (2000), an online journal, at www.biotechnews.com. Reprinted at www.sonicbloom.com/biotechnews.htm. You can read more about Sonic Bloom at www.sonicbloom.com.
7. See www.brainyquote.com/quotes/authors/t/thomas_a_edison.html.
8. Napoleon Hill, *Think and Grow Rich*, rev. ed. (San Diego, CA: Aventine Press, 2004), p. 107.
9. You can read more about the company at www.theangelconnection.org.
10. John Kanzius's story was first reported on CBS's *60 Minutes* on April 12, 2008. I found it on YouTube: www.youtube.com/watch ?v=BkzCSNTYWXg.
11. Excite@Home became a casualty of the Internet bubble of 2000 and filed for bankruptcy. Blue Mountain Arts was sold by Excite and is now an affiliate of American Greetings Corp. It still has one of the most popular greeting card sites on the Internet. From the Motley Fool website, www.fool.com/portfolios/rulebreaker/1999/rulebreaker/991025.htm, and www.bluemountain.com
12. Joseph Campbell with Bill Moyers, *The Power of Myth* (New York: Random House, 1988), p. 150; Adam Smith and Edwin Cannan, *An Inquiry Into the Nature and Causes of the Wealth of Nations* (1904; reprint, Chicago: University of Chicago Press, 1976), p. 477.

CHAPTER 4. ELIMINATING COUNTERFEIT CURRENCY

1. Gary Zukav has a three-year program called "Authentic Power," in which I am enrolled. For more information, visit his website: www.seatofthesoul.org.
2. John Bradshaw, *Homecoming* (New York: Bantam, 1992), p. 5.

CHAPTER 5. ADVENTUREPRISE

1. You can read more about Michelle Whitedove at www.michelle whitedove.com.

2. The Science of Mind is a teaching based around *The Science of Mind: A Philosophy, A Faith, A Way of Life* by Ernest Holmes (New York: McBride and Co., 1938; reprint, New York: Penguin Putnam, 1998).

3. See Laura Duksta's websites, www.lauraduksta.com and www.hippie andthebaldchick.com.

4. Statistics on autism courtesy of Autism Today, www.autismtoday.org. For further reading on this subject, see Karen L. Simmons et al., *Little Rain Man: Autism through the Eyes of a Child* (Arlington, TX: Future Horizons, 1996); and Jack Canfield et al., *Chicken Soup for the Soul: Children with Special Needs, Stories of Love and Understanding for Those Who Care for Children with Disabilities* (Deerfield Beach, FL: Health Communications, 2007).

5. The information about his history has been gathered from my own conversations with the medium, João Teixeira de Faria, and interviews with numerous local mediums at the casa, *pousada* (the Portuguese word for a lodge or hotel) owners, taxi drivers, and tour guides. See also www.friendsofthecasa.com.

6. See the Locks of Love website, www.locksoflove.org/history.html.

7. Susan Harrow, *The Ultimate Guide to Getting Booked on Oprah* (Oakland, CA: Harrow Communications, 2004), was a source for some of the background information on Oprah Winfrey. See the website www.prsecrets.com.

8. See http://inventors.about.com/library/inventors/blpostit.htm.

9. See http://inventors.about.com/library/inventors/blpopsicle.htm.

10. Marianne Williamson, *A Return to Love* (New York: HarperCollins, 1995), p. 191.

CHAPTER 6. YOUR STAKEHOLDERS

1. Edwin S. Rubenstein, ESR Research, "Educating Illegals Costs $900 per American Child," February 24, 2004, available at www.vdare.com/rubenstein/educating_illegals.htm (accessed May 6, 2008).

2. The Open Era in tennis began in 1968. Prior to that, only amateur players were permitted to compete in mainstream tennis competitions, including Grand Slam events. Professional tennis players competed in separate championship events.

3. If you would like to watch Andre Agassi's tearful retirement speech, the video is available for viewing at YouTube.com. Also, you can read

more about the Andre Agassi Charitable Foundation at www.agassi foundation.org.

4. The individuals in the research studies conducted at Maharishi University were trained in the technique of Transcendental Meditation. For more information on the subject of how group intention establishes coherent energy fields, see the research at the Permanent Peace website, www.permanentpeace.org.

5. This quotation comes from the Reverend David Owen Ritz's audio program *Keys to the Kingdom*, which he promotes via his website, www.davidowenritz.com.

6. See the Global Youth Action Network website, www.youthlink.org/gyanv5/index.htm.

7. Source: Kiva website, www.kiva.org.

8. I found these lines from Rabindranath Tagore quoted on the website www.theschoolofwisdom.com.

9. From the home page of the Ashoka website, www.ashoka.org.

10. See http://beenthere.typepad.com/been_there/2007/09/index.html. I also heard Bill Drayton's speech live at the Clinton Global Initiative Conference, where he told the original story that has been reported elsewhere.

11. Read more about the Gaia Community at www.gaia.com/community.

12. Information about the Academy of Management can be found at www.aomonline.org, and about the Association of Fundraising Professionals at www.afpnet.org.

13. Read more about Whispering Stars Web Design at www.whispering stars.com, and about Daniel Nahmod at www.danielnahmod.com.

14. Dr. Jean Houston teaches a program for social artistry. See her website for more details: www.jeanhouston.com.

CHAPTER 7. SOUL CURRENCY "MAGIC"

1. Jon Kabat-Zinn, Center for Mindfulness in Medicine, Health Care, and Society, at the University of Massachusetts Medical School in Worcester, www.umassmed.edu/Content.aspx?id=41252.

2. The Institute of HeartMath, www.heartmath.org.

3. Stephen G. Post is a professor of bioethics and family medicine in the School of Medicine, Case Western Reserve University, Cleveland. He served as a senior research scholar in the Becket Institute at Saint

Hugh's College, Oxford University. He is also president of the Institute for Research on Unlimited Love, which was founded in 2001 with a generous grant from the John Templeton Foundation. See www.unlimitedloveinstitute.org.

4. See the Stress, Humour, and Health website, www.chy.com.au/patch.htm.

5. See the Stress, Humour, and Health website, www.chy.com.au.

6. See the Stress, Humour, and Health website, www.chy.com.au.

7. Joyzelle Davis, "High Tea with Mo Siegel: Former Celestial Boss Talks about Whole Foods, His Investment Firm, Improving Lives," *Rocky Mountain News*, November 3, 2007.

8. From the Celestial Seasonings website, http://celestialseasonings.mediaroom.com/index.php?s=press_releases&item=39.

9. See the Whole Foods Market website, www.wholefoodsmarket.com/company/history.html.

10. Muriel Strode, *At the Roots of Grasses* (New York: Moffat, Yard, and Company, 1923). This quote is often erroneously attributed to Ralph Waldo Emerson.

SUGGESTIONS FOR *SOUL CURRENCY* STUDY GROUPS

1. Mastermind groups are usually groups of two or more people who get together regularly to further their goals and visions. Through a process developed by the late Rev. Jack Boland, a Unity minister, masterminding is a process of prayer, support, and visioning. The term has also often been used loosely to describe other mutual support groups.

RECOMMENDED READING

While I believe that *Soul Currency* offers a full and complete program, it would also be possible to write an entire book expanding on the subject matter in each chapter. Further insights can be gained by reading some of the books recommended below, which are the best ones available on the following topics. I have admired these authors, both as teachers and writers, and I am grateful for their contributions to my journey.

CAPITAL AND FLOW

Butterworth, Eric. *Spiritual Economics: The Principles and Process of True Prosperity*. Unity Village, MO: Unity House, 1993.

Cohen, Don, and Laurence Prusak. *In Good Company: How Social Capital Makes Organizations Work*. Cambridge, MA: Harvard University Press, 2001.

Csikszentmihaly, Mihaly. *Finding Flow: The Psychology of Engagement with Everyday Life*. New York: Basic Books, 1997.

DeMartini, John F. *How to Make One Hell of a Profit and Still Get to Heaven*. Carlsbad, CA: Hay House, 2004.

Eker, T. Harvey. *Secrets of the Millionaire Mind: Mastering the Inner Game of Wealth*. New York: HarperCollins, 2005.

Gage, Randy. *Why You're Dumb, Sick, and Broke: And How to Get Smart, Healthy, and Rich*. Miami, FL: Prime Concepts Group, 2001.

Harmony, Diane. *Five Gifts for an Abundant Life: Create a Consciousness of Wealth*. Encinitas, CA: Universal Harmony House, 2004.

Nemeth, Maria. *The Energy of Money: A Spiritual Guide to Financial and Personal Fulfillment*. New York: Ballantine, 1999.

Ponder, Catherine. *The Dynamic Laws of Prosperity: Forces That Bring Riches to You*. Englewood Cliffs, NJ: Prentice-Hall, 1962.

Tapscott, Don, and Anthony D. Williams. *Wikinomics: How Mass Collaboration Changes Everything*. New York: Portfolio/Penguin, 2006.

Twist, Lynne, with Teresa Barker. *The Soul of Money: Transforming Your Relationship with Money and Life*. New York: W. W. Norton, 2003.

Zohar, Dana, and Ian Marshal. *Spiritual Capital: Wealth We Can Live By*. London: Bloomsbury Publishing, 2004.

SCIENCE AND SPIRITUALITY

Braden, Gregg. *The Divine Matrix: Bridging Time, Space, Miracles, and Belief*. Carlsbad, CA: Hay House, 2007.

Dossey, Larry. *Healing Words: The Power of Prayer and the Practice of Medicine*. New York: HarperCollins, 1993.

———. *Prayer Is Good Medicine: How to Reap the Healing Benefits of Prayer*. New York: HarperCollins, 1996.

Emoto, Masaru. *The Hidden Messages in Water*. Hillsboro, OR: Beyond Words Publishing, 2004.

Gardner, Howard. *Frames of Mind: The Theory of Multiple Intelligences*. New York: Basic Books, 1993.

Goleman, Daniel. *Destructive Emotions: A Scientific Dialogue with the Dalai Lama*. New York: Bantam Dell Publishing, 2003.

———. *Emotional Intelligence: Why It Can Matter More Than IQ*. New York: Bantam Books, 1997.

Goswami, Amit. *The Self-Aware Universe: How Consciousness Creates the Material World*. New York: Jeremy P. Tarcher/Putnam, 1995.

Holmes, Ernest. *This Thing Called You*. New York: Jeremy P. Tarcher/Putnam, 1948.

Seligman, Martin E. *Learned Optimism: How to Change Your Mind and Your Life*. New York: Simon and Schuster, 2001.

Senge, Peter, et al. *Human Purpose and the Field of the Future*. Cambridge, MA: Society for Organizational Learning, 2004.

INTENTIONALITY AND TRANSFORMATION

Campbell, Joseph. *Myths to Live By*. New York: Viking Press, 1973.

Canfield, Jack, and Mark Victor Hansen. *The Aladdin Factor*. New York: Berkley, 1995.

Dwoskin, Hale. *The Sedona Method: Your Key to Lasting Happiness, Success, Peace, and Emotional Well-Being*. Sedona, AZ: Sedona Press, 2003.

Dyer, Wayne W. *Change Your Thoughts — Change Your Life: Living the Wisdom of the Tao*. Carlsbad, CA: Hay House, 2007.

———. *The Power of Intention: Learning to Co-Create Your World Your Way*. Carlsbad, CA: Hay House, 2004.

Grason, Sandy. *Journalution: Journaling to Awaken Your Inner Voice, Heal Your Life, and Manifest Your Dreams*. Novato, CA: New World Library, 2005.

Losier, Michael J. *The Law of Attraction: The Science of Attracting More of What You Want and Less of What You Don't*. New York: Hachette Book Group, 2006.

McTaggart, Lynne. *The Intention Experiment: Using Your Thoughts to Change Your Life and the World*. New York: Free Press, 2007.

SPIRITUAL ASSETS AND LOVE

Dalai Lama. *The Compassionate Life*. Boston, MA: Wisdom Publications, 2003.

Duksta, Laura. *I Love You More*. Naperville, IL: Sourcebooks Trade, 2007.

Hendricks, Gay. *Conscious Living: Finding Joy in the Real World*. New York: HarperCollins, 2000.

Hicks, Esther, and Jerry Hicks. *The Astonishing Power of Emotions: Let Your Feelings Be Your Guide*. Carlsbad, CA: Hay House, 2007.

Jampolsky, Gerald G. *Teach Only Love: Twelve Principles of Attitudinal Healing*. Rev. ed. Tulsa, OK: Council Oak Books, 2004.

Whitehouse, Maureen. *Soul-Full Eating: A (Delicious) Path to Higher Consciousness*. Hollywood, FL: Axiom Publishing, 2007.

Williamson, Marianne. *A Return to Love: Reflections on the Principles of a Course in Miracles*. New York: HarperCollins, 1992.

Zukav, Gary. *Soul to Soul: Communications from the Heart*. New York: Free Press, 2007.

FOLLOWING YOUR PASSION

Houston, Jean. *A Mythic Life: Learning to Live Our Greater Story*. New York: HarperCollins, 1996.

LeBlanc, Donna. *The Passion Principle: Discover Your Personal Passion Signature and the Secrets to Deeper Relationships in Love, Life, and Work*. Deerfield Beach, FL: Health Communications, 2005.

Levoy, Gregg. *Callings: Finding and Following an Authentic Life*. New York: Three Rivers Press, 1997.

Terkel, Studs. *Working: People Talk about What They Do All Day and How They Feel about What They Do*. New York: New Press, 1997.

Wood, John. *Leaving Microsoft to Change the World: An Entrepreneur's Odyssey to Educate the World's Children*. New York: HarperCollins, 2006.

MANAGING YOUR ADVENTUREPRISE

Chappell, Tom. *The Soul of a Business: Managing for Profit and the Common Good*. New York: Bantam, 1996.

Ferrazzi, Keith, with Tahl Raz. *Never Eat Alone: And Other Secrets to Success, One Relationship at a Time*. New York: Doubleday/Random House, 2005.

Gerber, Michael. *The E-Myth Revisited: Why Most Small Businesses Don't Work and What to Do about It*. New York: HarperCollins, 2001.

Ray, Michael, and Rochelle Myers. *Creativity in Business*. New York: Doubleday, 1989.

MISCELLANEOUS

Chopra, Deepak. *The Seven Spiritual Laws of Success: A Practical Guide to Fulfillment of Your Dreams*. Novato, CA: New World Library/Amber-Allen, 1994.

De Angelis, Barbara. *How Did I Get Here?* New York: St. Martin's Press, 2005.

Dooley, Mike. *Notes from the Universe: New Perspectives from an Old Friend*. Orlando, FL: TUT Enterprises, 2003.

Jampolsky, Gerald. *Shortcuts to God*. Berkeley, CA: Ten Speed Press, 2000.

Rann, Michael C., and Elizabeth Rann Arrott. *Shortcut to a Miracle: How to Change Your Consciousness and Transform Your Life*. Santa Monica, CA: Jeffers Press, 2006.

INDEX

ABOUT THE AUTHOR

Accomplished entrepreneur Ernest D. Chu has been a spiritual teacher for the past decade. Prior to that, he had a distinguished thirty-year career in finance, including as an allied member of the New York Stock Exchange, an investment banking executive, and a capital markets expert. He has advised some of America's largest companies and has raised capital for hundreds of public- and private-growth companies in a variety of industries. As an entrepreneur, he funded or was a member of the founding executive team of nine companies, three of which went public. He has raised more than $150 million for these and other client companies, and he has generated more than $1 billion in market capitalization value.

He began teaching spiritual abundance courses at the Center for Spiritual Living in Fort Lauderdale, Florida, where he has served as a trustee for more than ten years. He was licensed as a staff minister in 1999. In 2004, he became the Center's assistant pastor, and he was ordained in 2006. Through the Soul Currency Institute, he coaches socially and environmentally responsible entrepreneurs and companies.

Chu has published dozens of articles on corporate finance and entrepreneurship in such publications as the *Wall Street Journal, Corporate Finance Week, MBA* magazine, and the *Palm Beach Times*, and he has contributed to three business anthologies on finance, venture capital, and entrepreneurship. His articles on abundance and personal wisdom frequently appear on blogs and in a variety of personal growth and business magazines.

His website is www.soulcurrency.org.